Praise for
Guarding the Child's Imagination

It is no surprise, to parents today, that the world we live in now is not our grandparents' world. As things become darker around us, we must be diligent and use discernment in raising our children with Godly wisdom. Be prepared for your eyes to be opened and discover what the enemy is doing by first-hand accounts this author shares in her book. This book offers hope to those who desire to know and understand the spiritual implications of what our children are exposed to and how we, as parents, can do something about it. Influence is everything. Who and what your children are exposed to matters. What you will find in this book will be a beacon of light in these dark times. Please pray for the children and those who teach them. The author of this book is one of the great teachers who pray for your children and help them in the classroom in ways few are equipped to do.

—**Paula Wade,** Graduate of Charis Bible College, Minister of the Gospel of Jesus Christ

***

In this book, Denise provides real-world stories of how she was able to intercede on behalf of children. I found that I was able to pull valuable tips from every chapter that applied to my children. We have homeschooled all four of our children, from day one for over 12 years now, for the very reasons this book describes. Whether you homeschool or have children in public school, this book will be an eye-opener. We can all learn from Denise's experience in the classroom.

The best advice I can give is to get this book and follow the examples Denise has set for us. There is not a single home or school that should be without it. This book will bless you and your family for generations if you apply the recommendations.

—**Mark Priess**, Homeschool Parent

***

This masterfully composed book was created to address the questions that parents and educators have while striving to shape the minds of today's youth. A myriad of organic and material influences are skillfully converging to impede progress across all aspects of today's youth development. Drawing on her experiences as a parent and educator, Denise White offers transformative insights that can not only help resolve issues but also cultivate successful relationships with the children in one's life.

—**Pastor David Jordan**, Senior Pastor, Ultimate Faith Christian Center

***

"Guarding the Child's Imagination" reveals how vulnerable a child's imagination is in today's world and how easily a young mind can be influenced and have a negative impact on the child's growth and development. The author provides many real examples of children sharing dark thoughts that can damage a child's innocent thoughts. This book introduces readers to concepts that are easy to understand and based on biblical truths that support the author's unique encouragement that will help you become a better parent.

—**James White**

Guarding the Child's Imagination

Called to Truth Series, Book 3

Denise White

Published by KHARIS PUBLISHING, an imprint of KHARIS MEDIA LLC.

Copyright © 2025 Denise White

ISBN-13: 978-1-63746-316-1
ISBN-10: 1-63746-316-2

Library of Congress Control Number: 2025934275

All rights reserved. This book or parts thereof may not be reproduced in any form, stored in a retrieval system, or transmitted in any form by any means - electronic, mechanical, photocopy, recording, or otherwise - without prior written permission of the publisher, except as provided by United States of America copyright law.

All KHARIS PUBLISHING products are available at special quantity discounts for bulk purchase for sales promotions, premiums, fund-raising, and educational needs. For details, contact:
Kharis Media LLC
Tel: 1-630-909-3405
support@kharispublishing.com
www.kharispublishing.com

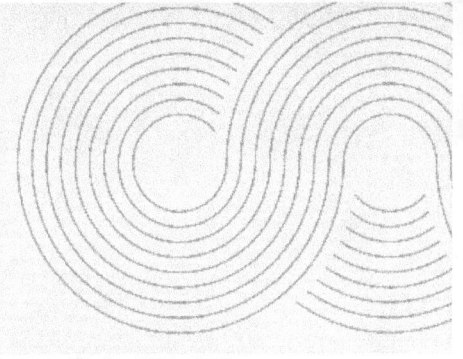

ACKNOWLEDGMENT

One of the greatest joys of my life is being a mother. I am grateful to my children for their love and the precious time we spend together. I am grateful to all the children I have met and had the pleasure of sharing a relationship with. Children are an incredibly precious gift from God. They have taught me to hope more, laugh more, listen more, love more, and stop and smell the roses.

I praise the LORD for His faithfulness in my life, His power and strength, and for leading me to the truth. Jesus said, "*I am the way, the truth, and the life: no man comes to the Father, but by Me.*" I am grateful to God for my husband of 36 years who has been on this journey of truth and life with me. God is the giver of life and has healed my husband and kept him alive through two near-death events in the last year. My husband says, "God has saved my life too many times to count!"

MY BELIEFS

I believe the Bible is the Word of God and the power and authority of believers. I believe in God the Father. I believe in Jesus Christ as my Lord and Savior, and He is the Son of God. He lived a sinless life on earth and died on the cross for the sins of the world. He rose from the dead. He conquered sin, death, disease, and Satan. Through Jesus Christ's completed work on the cross, we are saved, healed, delivered, preserved, and made whole. I believe in the Holy Spirit. As a disciple of Jesus Christ, I walk by faith, not by sight! By the power of the Holy Spirit, I walk in victory and overcome! *"And they overcome him (Satan) by the blood of the Lamb, and by the word of their testimony; and they loved not their lives to the death."* (Revelation 12:11)

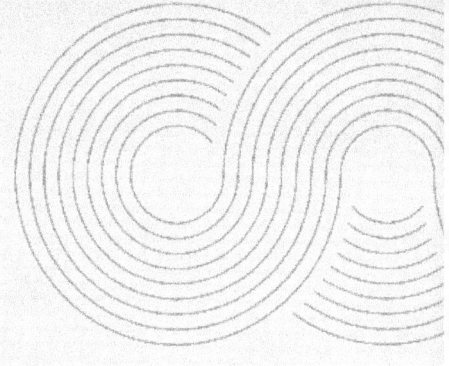

PURPOSE AND DISCLAIMER

This book is intended to help guide parents, grandparents, guardians, or others who influence children. It is meant to bring truth and light to those who influence children. This book was written to assist parents in understanding the spiritual aspects of their child and the effect it has on their imagination and mind. It is not intended to provide medical advice or professional counseling. This book is not intended to take the place of medical treatment or professional counseling. Always consult with your medical health care provider or professional counselor before making any change to you or your child's physical regimen regarding fasting, medication, diet, or any treatment. This book is not a substitute for medical care, advice, diagnosis, treatment, or professional counseling.

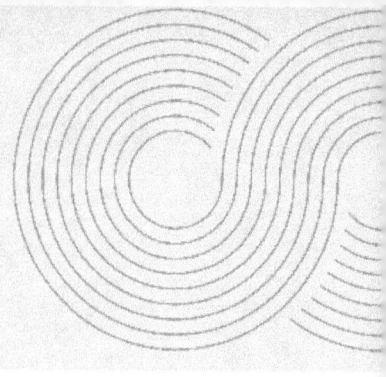

CONFIDENTIALITY

All the names used in my personal stories have been changed to protect the privacy of the person. When needed, story details may have been slightly changed to protect other's privacy.

INTRODUCTION

Our responsibility as parents is to do our best in raising our children according to the LORD's principles of the Bible. When we humbly follow the LORD, we will learn and grow from Him. He will teach us His ways and how to guide our children into all truth. *"But Jesus called them to Himself, saying (to the apostles), 'Allow the children to come to Me, and do not forbid them, for the kingdom of God belongs to such as these.'"* (Luke 18:16)

My hope for this book is to encourage you and your family to practice your spiritual discernment which includes teaching your children to cast off evil thoughts and imaginations. *"Casting down imaginations, and every high thing that exalts itself against the knowledge of God, and bringing into captivity every thought to the obedience of Christ."* (2Corinthians 10:5)

TABLE OF CONTENTS

Acknowledgment .... *vii*

My Beliefs .... *viii*

Purpose And Disclaimer .... *ix*

Confidentiality .... *x*

Introduction .... *xi*

Chapter 1: Guarding The Imagination 15

Chapter 2: The Power Of The Imagination 27

Chapter 3: The Age Of Accountability 33

Chapter 4: Beware Of Fairytales, Fables, Myths, And Traditions 39

Chapter 5: The Occult 47

Chapter 6: Shining The Light On The Darkness Of Video Game Addiction 51

Chapter 7: The Seared Conscience 59

Chapter 8: A Sound Mind 63

Chapter 9: Renewing The Child's Mind 73

Chapter 10: Protecting The Child's Senses And Their Soul 77

Chapter 11: Testing The Source 81

Chapter 12: Standing Guard For The Children 91

Chapter 13: Not Lowering Our Standards For Our Children... 97

Chapter 14: Teaching Children The Truth.... 107

Chapter 15: Words Matter.............................. 117

Chapter 16: The Power Of A Story 119

Chapter 17: Who Is Influencing Your Child? 123

Chapter 18: Bringing Peace To The Children 127

Chapter 19: Nurturing The Child's Imagination 135

Chapter 20: Not Hindering The Children From The Kingdom 141

Chapter 21: Restoring Order To The Child's Mind And Soul.. 147

Chapter 22: Be An Influencer 153

Conclusion-Action Plan............................... 155

Bibliography.. 159

CHAPTER 1
GUARDING THE IMAGINATION

My roles in the classroom have varied from teacher, substitute teacher (guest teacher), reading interventionist, and classroom specialist. There are many interesting students and situations I have experienced and learned from, which you will get to hear about throughout these chapters. This particular school day involved a fifth-grade student who was visibly upset and seemed tormented. He wanted to go to the school psychologist and therefore I sent him there, but he still came back upset. I asked him what was wrong, and he said his grandfather recently died and last night he was preparing for the next day to attend his grandfather's celebration of life. He was telling me he didn't get to spend a lot of time with his grandfather and that his mind wouldn't shut off about it, and he wasn't able to stop his racing thoughts. I told him he does have control over his thoughts, and he can tell the lies and the torment to stop. We had a conversation about this, and then he said okay and agreed with me. We discussed a little bit about the memories he had with his grandfather, instead of talking about the regret the demons were trying to plant in his mind. This boy did have good memories of his grandfather; they spent summers together fishing and riding bikes. After telling me about some of his good memories, he realized he did have a lot to share about his grandfather at the celebration of life. In a very simplistic way, I was trying to teach this boy how to cast off the evil imagination Satan was putting in his mind. We are to tell the lie to "STOP" aloud. The words we speak produce life or death. Jesus used scripture to stop the lies of Satan when He was in the wilderness and tempted by Satan, and this is our example to follow.

The next school day included a second-grade classroom, and a little girl named Dani who cried repeatedly in the classroom. Her friends kept trying to console her, but the crying continued. I asked her what was wrong and after some discussion, she told me she had been having repeated nightmares of her mom getting hurt. I told her these thoughts were lies. I told her to speak to these imaginations (dreams) and told her to say "STOP" to them. I was trying to teach her to command the evil thoughts to stop. We don't say please to Satan but command him to leave us alone. Jesus said, "Get behind me, Satan!" I prayed for Dani as I went back to my desk.

We need to be teaching children about the authority they have over their imagination, thoughts, and dreams. We need to be teaching children about the power of their agreement and that they have power in their words to stop the evil imaginations coming into their thoughts and dreams. We need to teach our children about the power of their words and what they agree with. They need to be taught scripture so they can pray spiritual warfare prayers; dear Heavenly Father, your word says that no weapon formed against me will prosper and every tongue that shall rise against me in judgment, I shall condemn. This is the heritage of the servants of the LORD, and their righteousness is of Me, says the LORD. I pray this in Jesus' name. Amen.

At the end of the school day, a seven-year-old standing in the bus line looked at me and said, "My mind is dark". This boy went on to talk about a movie star who keeps making dark movies, and he told me with an upset voice how he didn't understand why an actor would continue to make such dark movies. It was quite evident that this boy had watched these disturbing movies, and he wanted to stop thinking about them because of the evil thoughts they were putting in his head. I had little time with this troubled boy, but he had a choice not to watch the movies and I had a choice to pray for him. I pray that this little boy and his parents come to the knowledge of the truth. We need to teach children to listen to their conscience and not discount that inner voice of the Holy Spirit speaking to their spirit.

Today I was in a third-grade classroom where the teacher had made a "Bag of Torture" where the students drew from the bag to receive good or bad rewards. Why do you think this is a bad idea? If we lead children into thinking they should be tortured, then it could lead to lies in their mind and normalize the oppression Satan wants to cause in their lives. It could cause the child to normalize things in their mind that are evil and wrong. We don't want our children to think it is alright to be oppressed by Satan. We want to teach them to fight back with the spiritual principles in the Bible. They need to know there is a spiritual battle. The Bible says we are not to be ignorant of Satan's devices and that includes our children.

As we continue looking at the imagination of the child and what children are exposed to, we will take a look into a 3rd-grade classroom where I was teaching as a guest teacher. It was time for a student to read a book of his choice. The student took his seat in the rocking chair at the head of the classroom, and as I was listening to the child read, the story was all about cauldrons and magic potions. This is the same classroom where they had an elf on the shelf and students were extremely expressive that no one could touch the elf, or he would disappear and fly away. There was a ritual at the beginning of class that this classroom followed; they did a pinky swear to promise to be responsible and kind. These things may seem innocent at first glance if you ignore the spiritual implications of things. But in truth, these things are divination and are not okay according to biblical principles. A lot of these types of activities may seem like fun and games but are a slippery slope as they teach children to use their imagination in ways that cause confusion and lead them to agree with things that are not truth but lies and of Satan. It seems very wrong when children know more about the powers of a make-believe elf than the power of the Lord Jesus

Christ. It is amazing how children across our nation know all about the imaginary land of the North Pole, Santa Claus, and the elves. Teaching our children imaginary stories can be quite damaging to the conscience. If children learn that their imagination is for fun and games and not for a good purpose, we lose important opportunities to teach them how valuable their imagination can be. What about teaching our children to use their imagination to think on truths of God's word instead of training their imaginations to meditate on fairytales, lies, and deceptions?

Are our children's imaginations on the gods of this world? Who are the gods of this world? Some of the gods of this world are Greek gods, Easter Bunny over the resurrection of Jesus Christ, Santa Claus over the birth of Jesus Christ, greed of shopping over the power of giving, having a heart of greed instead of a heart of love, idolizing people or ourselves, lust for earthly power, pride, etc.

Children's imaginations are very precious and must be guarded. Let's take a look at the interest in vampire books and movies. The world's view of vampires is that it is entertainment. There have been well-known books, movies, and television shows on vampires. Some of these have been popular amongst teenagers. What is essentially wrong with these books and movies? Let's see what the Bible says about this topic. First of all, let's look at Leviticus 17:10-12. In my King James Version Easy Reading, these verses are red letters meaning God is speaking. *"And whatsoever man there be of the house of Israel, or of the strangers that sojourn (stay) among you, that eats any manner of blood; I will even set My face against that soul that eats blood and will cut him off from among his people. For the life of the flesh is in the blood: I have given it to you upon the altar to make an atonement for your souls: for it is the blood that makes an atonement for the soul."* Secondly, Deuteronomy 12:23, *"Only be sure that you eat not the blood: for the blood is the life; and you may not eat the life with the flesh (meat)."* Lastly, in Proverbs 30:15, is the word "horseleech" which comes from the Hebrew word 'Alukah' which means blood-lusting monster or vampire. What does the world say about the traits of a vampire; they thirst for blood, they are back from the dead, they are hypersensitive to the sunlight, appear to be immune to injury, reproduction by biting, superhuman ability, amazing speed, susceptible to stakes, characteristic of having fangs, and fire destroys them. What is interesting to me is that the vampire traits seem like demonic traits and demons hate the fire of God similar to vampires. Again, Satan wants children to believe demons, vampires, etc. are harmless because then he can easily trick children when they are being entertained by Satan's books, movies, fantasy role-playing games, video games, etc. In conclusion, children are not to drink or eat blood because life is in the blood; therefore, these vampire beings are not to be entertained. We know as believers that light and darkness have nothing in common and according to Ephesians 5:13, all things are exposed by the light. Many of the traits of vampires align with demonic spiritual beings. We are to remove evil objects and the demonic attached to them according to Deuteronomy

7:25-26. What does this scripture say? *"You shall burn the carved images of their gods with fire; you shall not covet the silver or gold that is on them, nor take it for yourselves, lest you be snared by it; for it is an abomination to the LORD your God. Nor shall you bring an abomination into your house, lest you be doomed to destruction like it. You shall utterly detest it and utterly abhor it, for it is an accursed thing."* We need to spiritually clean our houses of all Satan-inspired items.

What do parents need to know about protecting their children from witchcraft and divination? Let's look at what Focus on the Family says in an article titled "Witchcraft: What Christian Parents Need to Know". Here are two quotes from the article: *"The world of witchcraft is similar because there is a very real seduction that takes place. Maybe it starts with things that are often seen as fun and games. Reading your horoscopes. Playing with a Ouija board at a party. Participating in a TikTok trend that is really just a spell in disguise. Please understand, it's everywhere. It's at the local mall or at your local Barnes & Noble. It is all over social media. And the enemy isn't dumb. He makes his lies very appealing. Especially to young people."* Additionally, the article discusses how witchcraft can be a particular draw for young women. This article explains that *"It's critical for parents and spiritual leaders to help young women understand how unique and beautiful they are and inspire them to discover who God created them to be."* It is a wonderful adventure for a child to discover who they are and explore their interests and giftings. The LORD created each child uniquely, and it is exciting to explore each child's uniqueness. Children need to be told they are special because each child has been carefully and lovingly designed by their Creator. They were knit in their mother's womb by Almighty God and created for a plan and a purpose. There is a specific purpose for each child to walk into.

Let's continue our investigation into the imagination of the child. I was a guest teacher in a second-grade classroom, and I was using the whiteboard to show the math problems. There was an elf (on the shelf) on the whiteboard near where I was writing. Apparently, I came close to touching the elf or possibly actually touched it, and the whole class screamed "You touched the elf". Later, I asked a student from the class, "Why did the students scream when I came close to the elf." The student said, "The elf will lose its powers and fly away." I was unaware of the elf on the shelf fairytale. These fairytales, specifically The Elf on the Shelf, teach children to have imaginary friends which can be Satan's way of training them and to gain access into their imaginations. Satan wants us and children to think these fairytales and traditions are just fun entertainment. Let's examine the "Elf on the Shelf" fairytale. Apparently, the Elf on the Shelf is a toy based on a children's book published in 2005. According to this fairytale, when a child names the elf, it magically comes to life. This tradition is done from Thanksgiving to Christmas. This fairytale states that the elf will report to Santa the child's behavior. The elf moves to a new location each night which is the responsibility of the parent to relocate it each night while the children are led to believe it moved magically. The last part of the fairytale is that if the child touches the elf, it will lose its magic. An article from Children's Health discussed the possible danger of the Elf on the Shelf being a lie and therefore threatening the trustworthiness of the parents. It also mentioned the possibility of it encouraging the gullibility of children and that their good behavior should be governed by rewards at Christmas. The article stated what is most important is that families decide whether the tradition of the Elf on the Shelf is aligned with their own family values and religious faith.

Where did the celebration of Christmas originate and where did Santa Claus originate? From History.com, *"The Christian holiday of Christmas, especially, owes many of its traditions to the ancient Roman festival, including the time of year Christmas is celebrated."* Many of the traditions today from Western culture surrounding Christmas celebrations originated from Saturnalia such as gift giving, singing, lighting candles, and feasting. *"Saturnalia, held in mid-December, is an ancient Roman pagan festival honoring the agricultural god Saturn."* According to history.com, *"The legend of Santa Claus can be traced back hundreds of years to a monk named St. Nicholas."* Saint Nicholas became the subject of legends. *"Over the course of many years, Nicholas' popularity spread and became known as the protector of children and sailors."* Therefore, it seems sensible for each of us to evaluate for ourselves and our families how we choose to celebrate Christmas and Santa Claus. There is much more information out there on YouTube and articles for anyone who wishes to study these topics more thoroughly themselves if they so desire.

Denise White

What is the origin of Halloween? According to History.com, "*Halloween's origins date back to the ancient Celtic festival of Samhain (pronounced sow-in). The Celts, who lived 2,000 years ago, mostly in the area that is now Ireland, the United Kingdom, and northern France, celebrated their new year on November 1.*" The Celts celebrated Samhain on October 31 when they believed the ghosts of the dead returned to earth. They built large sacred bonfires where they burned animals and crops to sacrifice to their gods. They would wear costumes and tell fortunes. Therefore, from this tradition, Americans started dressing in costumes and going to neighborhood houses asking for money or food and eventually became a tradition of trick-or-treating. Thus, this is food for thought for us and our families, and do we want to celebrate this American tradition of Halloween? A fireman told me that the night before Halloween and on Halloween day, there would be cases of babies being sacrificed in the fire. There would also be cases of pregnant women giving birth, and the births were never reported. Additionally, I have observed recently in a subdivision that is mostly Christian residents an increase in very scary decorations such as large skeletons and demon-looking creatures that are about 14 feet tall or more displayed during October. Many dark events happen in October and on Halloween. What should we be doing in October? Should we be encouraging our children to be frightened and screaming until they are in tears and having nightmares?

Furthermore, as a teacher in kindergarten classrooms, all the way up to high school classrooms, I have seen an array of classroom activities. I have seen some classrooms with quite a large amount of witchcraft and sorcery items. This high school classroom had various pictures or plaques reading: "Not all witches live in Salem", "Do You Dare Enter the Witch's Lair", and "When I practice, I see results" this last sign had a picture of a magic wand. Other signs of divination in this classroom were brooms, crystals, and astrology items. Some people think these things are harmless and I used to be ignorant of this as well, but they are not harmless. We may have opened a door to the enemy. These items can open the door to the demonic. Demons can be attached to items. It is risky to display these items in our home or a classroom. This is why it is important to pray daily for a hedge of protection around our children since we don't always know what they are exposed to.

Can you imagine the truth that will manifest if we teach our children the principles of the kingdom of God instead of the imaginations of the world when they are young? If our children are taught God's biblical principles in their youth, can you imagine the better choices they would make and the truth that would manifest out of their mouths and lives?

In summary, we are to cast down evil imaginations instead of lulling the mind; listen to the Holy Spirit instead of seeking the words of psychics and divination; build up our family relationships more than being entertained by media; have family meals more than watching TV; serve and minister to the broken hearted instead of spending a lifetime of complacency. We are held responsible for our actions and how we handle the use of our time, including how we use our imagination. One school I taught at, had a very interesting announcement. The announcement to the students over the PA system said, *"Watch and control your thoughts, words, and actions."* This announcement brought to the students' attention that they have control over their thoughts.

What are we to celebrate, remember, and use our imagination to meditate on according to God's word? We are to think about those things that are true, honest, just, pure, lovely, of good report, virtuous, and anything praiseworthy. God's word says we are to take the Lord's Supper to remember (meditate on) what our Lord Jesus Christ did through His life, death, and resurrection. We are to meditate on the Word of God. According to Psalm 77:12, *"I will meditate also of all Thy work, and talk of thy doings."*

CHAPTER 2
THE POWER OF THE IMAGINATION

The power of our imagination allows us to visualize the Bible stories and bring them to life in our minds. God the Father, Jesus Christ, and the Holy Spirit are all spirits, and we cannot see them at present. Therefore, as we use our imagination to picture what the scripture is saying, it can be helpful. I know when I can't sleep at night, I picture that I am under the shelter of the Most High, and I fall peacefully asleep.

Our imagination is to be used for our good. My family needed and wanted to move, and I engaged my imagination by envisioning our life in our new location. I began planning and taking the necessary steps to move in that direction, I acknowledged the LORD, and I prayed He would direct our steps. A lot of planning for our futures begins in the imagination of our minds and hearts. Can we imagine ourselves here or there? Usually, before we ever make detailed plans for our life, we have already imagined ourselves in our final destination. If we haven't been able to picture ourselves at our final destination, it is almost impossible to plan our steps to get there. This also applies to children. Children need to use their imagination to move them forward in life in the right direction. I have seen children who have amazing imaginations but don't know how to use their imagination for good. Some children, if not led in the right direction, can escape their life difficulties by escaping into a fantasy world in their mind. Talking to our children about what is going on in their minds and hearts is essential to avoid becoming overwhelmed by life circumstances. Our children should be imagining what God has planned for them and not escaping into a fantasy world where perfection and a false reality exist. As His children, we will overcome many things in our lifetime when we follow Him. He wants the children's souls to prosper.

What is imagination? Let's review a few definitions, first from Oxford and second from Merriam Webster. First, the imagination: the faculty or action of forming new ideas, images, or concepts of external objects not present to the senses. Also, the imagination is the ability of the mind to be creative or resourceful. Secondly, the act or power of forming a mental image of something not present to the senses or never before wholly perceived in reality.

A fleeting thought comes and goes, but when we meditate on a thought and imagine in our minds, we are using our imagination. Fantasy is the activity of imagining things, especially things that are impossible or improbable. Merriam Webster's definition of fantasy is "the power or process of creating especially unrealistic or improbable mental images in response to psychological need". Notice the word "power"; there is power in our imaginations to create. This is why it is important to examine what we are meditating or imagining because we are creating something good or something bad. There are fantasy role playing games that can be very spiritually dangerous because they take your mind into a fantasy world that is not based on truth but a dark spiritual world. These games are not harmless games but Satan's game plans to deceive and draw people into depression, anger, recluse behavior, hopelessness, etc., and distract them from the plans God has for their life. If their destructive pattern continues, then before long, they can no longer even imagine what plans or purpose to aim towards. They, therefore, are not motivated. Their imagination can be seared similar to their conscience being seared. Satan wants to steal their creative ability to see their options and their talents by diverting God's plan. Satan wants to move children out of God's plan for their lives and into a path where he is controlling the child. His evil plan is to manipulate the child's mind, in order, that the child can no longer see God's vision for their life. It has recently come to my attention that a video game called Fortnite, that many children play, has a part of the game where you can sell your soul to the devil. In this game, you are actually negotiating with Satan. Our children have to be warned about these things that are trying to draw them to hell. Satan wants to normalize these things, so children think it is a game, but our souls are not a game to be played with.

Denise White

How do we discern the wicked imagination? Proverbs 6:18 says that the heart devises wicked imaginations. When we have a fleeting thought, this is not devising a wicked imagination. But when we spend time thinking on something and planning something in our thoughts and the intents of our heart, that is not God-pleasing, this is the wicked imagination. What can cause our imagination to be wicked? One root cause of an evil imagination is pride. We also must discern other's wicked imaginations. The LORD warns in Jeremiah 23 about prophets who speak out of the imagination of their own heart and say, "*no evil shall come upon you.*" We must discern what others say over our lives and not agree with deception.

Our imaginations have power whether it is good or evil. How are we to remove our evil imagination? Second Corinthians 10:3-5 says, "*For though we walk in the flesh, we do not war according to the flesh. For the weapons of our warfare are not carnal but mighty in God for pulling down strongholds, casting down arguments and every high thing that exalts itself against the knowledge of God, bringing every thought into captivity to the obedience of Christ.*" We do not argue with others or pridefully act out, but we fight spiritually. We battle our evil imaginations by taking authority over our own thoughts and speaking life with our mouth. We read and confess scripture and agree with His word. Jeremiah 7:24 says when we do not obey and listen to God but follow our evil imaginations, we go backwards in our life not forward.

What wrong thinking patterns have been formed through our family tree that now have been developed in our evil imagination? We may have been taught through our family tree to follow evil imaginations, and therefore, it is necessary to test our thoughts with the word of God. Jeremiah 9:14 says that men have walked after the imagination of their own heart and after Baalim which their fathers taught them. Our generational line may have taught us to follow traditions and superstitions that have become a pattern in our lives that are now a stronghold in our minds. These strongholds can derail our imaginations and lives and must be pulled down.

Have we lost our peace or have our children lost their peace? When our imaginations wander into wrong thinking, we can lose our peace. Isaiah 26:3 tells us how to keep our peace, *"You will keep him in perfect peace, whose mind is stayed on You, because he trusts in You."* If we have recognized we have lost our peace, we should evaluate what our imagination has been meditating on.

God knows what is going on in the heart of our imagination. In First Chronicles 28:9, David is talking to his son Solomon and explaining how God knows all the imaginations of the heart, *"And for you, my son Solomon, know the God of your father, and serve Him with a loyal heart and with a willing mind: for the LORD searches all hearts, and understands all the intents of the thoughts. If thou seek Him, He will be found by you; but if you forsake Him, He will cast you off forever."* Satan wants us to waste our minutes, hours, days, months, years, and decades on devising evil imaginations because then we are not serving God with a perfect heart.

Our imaginations are very powerful; therefore, we need to be mindful of what is going on in our imaginations. We are not to be mindlessly drifting into imagining any thoughts that come to our mind. We need to evaluate our thoughts and imagination continually, so we are not drawn into deceptions. In man's eyes, things may seem innocent, but God has a set of guidelines to protect us in His word. We must study His principles in scripture to protect our imagination and thoughts. Some may think it is innocent to wish upon a star but when we seek something or someone other than God for our future this is an occult practice. There are television shows and movies where someone is making a wish to an angel or a star. Should a child be using their imagination to ask an angel for a wish or to wish upon a star expecting their dreams to come true? When someone is wishing upon a star or asking an angel for a wish, these activities seek someone other than God for their future. When we follow biblical principles, we are following God's ways to bless and protect ourselves and our families. Leaning on anything other than God for our future can defile us which is to spoil. Therefore, guarding our imagination and what we are meditating on affects and directs the path we are headed down. Our imagination has the power to take our family into their predestined course or down a dead-end road. Don't allow your imagination to deter your family's destiny.

CHAPTER 3
THE AGE OF ACCOUNTABILITY

There is no exact age when a child knows right from wrong. God knows when a child has the understanding in their heart of right and wrong. *"Butter and honey shall he eat, that he may know to refuse the evil, and choose the good. For before the child shall know to refuse the evil, and choose the good, the land that thou dread will be forsaken by both her kings."* (Isaiah 7:15-16) Most parents will know when their child understands right from wrong. Another gauge to determine a child's age of accountability is puberty; the time of life when a child experiences physical and hormonal changes that mark a transition into adulthood. But there are exceptions to this guideline. As far as the morality of a child, once they know right from wrong and can say no to evil and be obedient to God, there is a type of "age of accountability". It is important to be praying for your child because if they are making bad decisions your prayers are battling against the evil trying to gain access to their mind and soul. It is vital while our children are under our roof and authority, that we do our best to teach them the LORD's ways and model the behavior of a child of God.

Let's look at more scripture verses and what they say about the age of accountability.

1) Proverbs 20:11 says, "*Even a child is known by his doings, whether his work be pure, and whether it be right.*"
2) Romans 14:12 says, "*So then every one of us shall give an account of himself to God.*"
3) According to Galatians 4:1-2, "*Now I say, That the heir, as long as he is a child, differs nothing from a servant (slave), though he be lord of all; But is under tutors (guardians) and governors (managers) until the time appointed of the father.*
4) Finally, James 4:17, "*Therefore to him that knows to do good, and does it not, to him it is sin.*" Therefore, once a child knows how to do good and doesn't do it, it is a sin for that child.

Why do I see so much turmoil in middle school-age children? It makes me wonder if it has something to do with the age of accountability. These children are growing into adults and are beginning to determine whether they will make wise choices or are heading down the wrong road. Satan walks around the earth seeking whom he can devour, and children are not exempt from this, and this is why the children cannot be ignorant of Satan's devices. Children cannot be ignorant of Satan's devices, especially the middle school children who are at the age of accountability or close.

From my personal experience of being in the middle and high school classrooms, the middle school student seems to be at a crossroads. Most of these middle school students, whose ages are anywhere between 11-14, are evaluating their choices and which path they will take. They are at or close to the age of accountability, which is when they know right from wrong and can make the right choice if they choose. There seems to be a lot more turmoil in the middle school ages versus the high school age groups. When I am in a high school classroom teaching, I generally see students who have already defined themselves in a specific group depending on who they identify with. Whereas in middle school, the students are in the process of figuring out who they are and what type of people they want to associate with.

There are all kinds of varying discussions I hear students talk about at school. One more recent discussion I heard in a middle school was about sexual orientation. They were discussing how to define themselves sexually and what their choices were. Satan has confused our youth and put thoughts in their imagination. Satan, who is known as the father of lies, has led our society into believing they can choose whether they should be a boy or a girl, or if they are heterosexual, homosexual, bisexual, or asexual. Satan is a liar and the father of them. God, Our Creator, made male and female and created marriage between one male and one female. Satan is always coming up with evil thoughts and imaginations to plant in people's minds, including our children. Therefore, this is why we need to be alert and cast-off evil imaginations. Some of Satan's evil ideas have been around since Satan was cast out of heaven and others are newer lies, but still LIES.

The last high school class I taught had a few students dressed in Gothic apparel and makeup. Their hair, make-up, and clothing were dark, and they each seemed sad when I looked at them. One student specifically stood out to me as she seemed particularly sad in class and had a large thick collar around her neck with round chains hanging from it. You really had to look twice and even three times to see her real eyes as they were disguised by these black oversized marks under her eyes, probably temporary tattoos that looked like large tears. She looked like she was in pain and despair. *"The eye is the lamp of the body. You draw light into your body through your eyes, and light shines out to the world through your eyes. So if your eye is well and shows you what is true, then your whole body will be filled with light. But if your eye is clouded or evil, then your body will be filled with evil and dark clouds. And the darkness that takes over the body of a child of God who has gone astray, that is the deepest, darkest darkness there is."* (Matthew 6:22-23 The Voice translation). When the Holy Spirit leads us into a child's life that needs truth, may we speak truth and life to them to set the captive free.

Don't forget, no matter how lost a child might be, the power of the blood of Jesus Christ of Nazareth and the name of Jesus, is above all other names. The name of Jesus is above the name of any disease, the name of Jesus is above any name of any mental oppression, and the name of Jesus is above any person's name that is bringing evil into a home. Jesus has overcome all evil, and now we as children of the God Most High must resist the enemy (Satan and his evil kingdom), and they will flee. Satan tempted Jesus three times and Jesus resisted each time by declaring the scriptures aloud. We overcome by the blood of the Lamb and the word of our testimony. What testimony are you speaking with your mouth? Are you testifying of how great your God is and declaring His truth?

CHAPTER 4
BEWARE OF FAIRYTALES, FABLES, MYTHS, AND TRADITIONS

What are the traditions of the world that deceive, trap, or simply waste our precious time? Colossians 2:8 says, *"Beware lest any man spoil you through philosophy and vain deceit, after the tradition of men, after the rudiments of the world, and not after Christ."* Furthermore, Mark 7:7-9 says, *"Howbeit in vain do they worship me, teaching for doctrines the commandments of men. For laying aside the commandment of God, you hold the traditions of men, as the washing of pots and cups and many other such things you do. And He said unto them, full well you reject the commandment of God, that you may keep your tradition."*

In the United States, we have many traditions of celebrating people and events which can cause some people to feel pressure to attend frequent celebrations when they have no desire to celebrate but feel forced into participating. If we put pressure on people to follow our man-made traditions and customs that the LORD does not require of us, we can cause someone to stumble who is not able to live up to these expectations.

Denise White

First of all, let's look at fables and fairytales. Fables are generally stories about animals, plants, or forces of nature that have humanlike characteristics. Fairytales are stories that involve magical characters and contain good and evil characters. First Timothy 1:4 says, *"Neither give heed to fables and endless genealogies, which minister questions, rather than godly edifying which is in faith: so do."* The definition of a fairytale is a children's story about magical and imaginary beings and lands. Synonyms for a fairytale are fairy story, folk tale, legend, myth, fantasy, or fiction. This definition of fairytale is very telling; a fairytale is a fabricated story especially one intended to deceive.

What does the word of God say about fables? Second Peter 1:16 says, *"For we have not followed cunningly devised fables, when we made known unto you the power and coming of our Lord Jesus Christ but were eyewitnesses of His majesty."* According to this scripture, fables are cleverly and deceitfully planned stories. Furthermore, First Timothy 4:7 says, *"But refuse profane and old wives' fables, and exercise thyself rather unto godliness."* According to this verse, fables are profanity and old wives' fables which are defined as a traditional belief that is not based on fact but superstition. In summary, fables are lies and are not to be listened to, followed, or taught to our children. Fables are profanity according to God's holy word. The Little Red Riding Hood fable has been around for hundreds of years and has different meanings and some of which are very disturbing. One of which is about the loss of innocence of a young girl. Some of the details surrounding the original meaning of Little Red Riding Hood were quite disturbing as I researched it. After we read these stories to children, why do some of them have nightmares? We don't always know the original meaning of fables and fairytales so why parents would want to tell their children these potentially disturbing stories when there is no benefit and can cause confusion in our children. Maybe we can make up our own creative stories with our children, and we could share Bible stories and discuss with our children their meaning.

What is the harm in reading fairytales and fables to our children? Have we ever contemplated what the fairytales and fables are teaching the little minds we are trying to nurture? We will begin with Hansel and Gretel. What are some of the concerning storylines in Hansel and Gretel? The wicked stepmother convinces the children's father to abandon his children in the woods. The witch in the story forces Gretel into slavery while deciding if Hansel is fat enough to eat. Let's look at the story of Snow White. Snow White's deceased mother's home is now home to her stepmother who is called wicked. The stepmother is a sorcerer. Snow White is poisoned after eating an apple given to her by the stepmother. Snow White is brought back to life magically by a kiss from a prince. Now let's look at the Pied Piper of Hamelin. The pied piper plays music that entices the children to follow him, and the children are put under a spell. The children followed the pied piper out of the town and disappeared. Moving on to the Little Mermaid. Ariel met a sea witch, and Ariel sacrificed her voice and her tongue to receive legs to walk. What about The Adventures of Pinocchio? In this story, children turn into donkeys and a wooden boy becomes human. Pinocchio gets kidnapped by a fox and a cat and gets sold to Geppetto. Beyond this, there are some very disturbing YouTube videos discussing some extremely dark parts of the Pinocchio movie version. In conclusion, we have just touched on a few of the fairytales and fables out there for children. We have seen these tales include magic, sorcery, abandonment, kidnapping, slavery, witches' spells, and deception. Looking at the big picture, do these stories benefit our children or do they confuse them and cause fear at a tender age?

A common theme within many childhood movies is the prince coming to rescue the princess. There are very few princesses or princes in the world, and the ones in the world don't frequently have a happy ever-after story. The idea that a prince is going to rescue a princess from all her troubles gives the wrong message. Young girls can become obsessed with these movies and can begin to build false beliefs in their heads at a young age. Also, many childhood movies have songs that become very popular and are memorized and sung repeatedly. For some children, these movies are not a problem but for other children, they begin to escape into a fantasy world that is easier to cope with than real life. They may be missing out on learning how to handle their emotions and may be missing out on learning how to handle real-life situations.

Let's investigate mythology. Mythology has been studied in schools for many years. Why have we been teaching something that is called a myth? Who initiated teaching myths in schools? *"Greek mythology is a body of stories concerning the gods, heroes, and rituals of the ancient Greeks"*. According to Encyclopedia Britannica, *"Although people of all countries, eras, and states of civilization have developed myths that explain the existence and workings of natural phenomena, recount the deeds of gods or heroes, or seek to justify social or political institutions, the myths of the Greeks have remained unrivaled in the Western world as sources of imaginative and appealing ideas."* Notice it says, "have developed myths that explain the existence and workings of natural phenomena, recount the deeds of gods". Shouldn't we be using our critical thinking to examine the teaching of mythology and what it is teaching our children? Mythology is taught in a lot of schools, usually beginning in middle school. It is necessary to have discussions in our homes about such myths.

When we teach our children from when they are little about fairytales, traditions, and myths and not the truth, their imaginations are being trained to escape into a dark realm of deception. Concerning teaching our children fairytales and traditions like Elf on the Shelf, we are training our children to have imaginary friends. The danger with this is that there is a real spiritual realm with good and evil fighting for their souls and that is not a myth. There are spiritual beings, called demons, that are trying to gain access to these little children's minds, and they are not imaginary friends but real dark spiritual beings. What about teaching our children about the spiritual realm that there is a real evil kingdom trying to inject lies into their minds, and that they can fight back in prayer.

A third-grade student, Stacie came to class one day, and we were talking about how beautiful the rainbow was outside. She said to me, "I didn't see the rainbow and I have never seen a rainbow before." I took her by the hand, and we went outside and saw the rainbow. We must teach our children the truths of the Bible and let them see them for themselves. The rainbow is a promise from God to never flood the earth again. This is the truth, not a fable or fairytale. At the time God flooded the earth, the Lord saw how great the wickedness of man was and how the thoughts of man were evil all the time. The sons of God (possibly fallen angels) came together with the daughters of men, and they bore children. This was unnatural and not the way God planned His creation. The times were quite evil and after the flood, the rainbow was a promise from God that He would not flood the earth again. But even though the rainbow is being used for other purposes today, God will not be mocked. The truths of scripture are not fables, fairytales, or myths. They are truths from our Creator to guide us into all truth and guide us into living a righteous and blessed life.

How and what to teach our children? Ultimately, God has entrusted us to teach our children. One thing I have learned from listening to students is that children need to be heard. They want someone to listen and not necessarily always have an answer to fix things but to have someone to listen to them. The power of being heard is very important because Satan wants to silence them, and God wants to help them become who He created them to be. Teaching children that they can talk to God at any time is of vital importance because He will be their best friend in life if they open the door and let Him in.

Are the children from Christian households, in America, more likely to recite movie lies than scripture verses? Shouldn't we be teaching children about the spiritual realm and the battle between good and evil because we are in this battle whether we want to be or not? Some children in our country are being trained for hours and hours each day to be sorcerers and witches in video games. What can we do to help the children in our nation and in our homes that have their imaginations held captive by Satan's evil? We are to pray for them, speak truth and life over them, and fight for our children with spiritual warfare. My best advice, from my personal experience, is to teach one truth at a time to a child when they are open to receiving it. It is one truth at a time that destroys one lie at a time.

CHAPTER 5
THE OCCULT

What are occult practices? When someone is following occult practices, they aren't trusting God with their future but looking elsewhere for spiritual insight that is not from God. Astrology and horoscopes are two examples of occult practices.

According to the Oxford Languages Dictionary, astronomy is *"the branch of science that deals with celestial objects, space, and the physical universe as a whole"*. Astrology is defined in the same dictionary as: *"the study of the movements and relative positions of celestial bodies interpreted as having an influence on human affairs and the natural world."* Therefore, it would seem reasonable that if we were studying the moon, stars, and sun to gain knowledge of their function and makeup, this seems to not be a problem. But when we begin to lean towards astrology and use the stars and celestial bodies to try and gain an understanding of ourselves and our future, this is treading on dangerous territory. The word of God is full of biblical principles that are for our protection and warn us about dangerous territory we are told to stay away from such as: making predictions as related to the moon, prophesying by the stars, listening to astrologers, seeking counsel from the celestial bodies for wisdom for your life (horoscopes), worshipping or serving the sun, moon, or stars. There are mysteries within God's creation and the universe that we may not understand but the word of God is clear about what we should stay away from.

I remember many years ago, horoscopes were in the newspaper. Today horoscopes are still found in the newspaper but in many other places also. Horoscopes are very accessible to people through books, newspapers, psychics, websites, social media, etc. The "zodiac sign" is the more common word used currently. According to Dictionary.com, "*the zodiac can be traced back to ancient civilizations, such as the ancient Greeks and Romans, who believed the position of heavenly bodies could be used to predict the future*". A common conversation amongst children on the playground is, "What is your zodiac sign?" Well, the word of God has something to say about astrology, and teaching the children what God says about astrology is necessary for them to follow the truth. In Isaiah 47:13-14, "*You are wearied in the multitude of your counsels. Let now the astrologers, the stargazers, the monthly prognosticators, stand up, and save you from these things that shall come upon you. Behold, they shall be as stubble; the fire shall burn them; they shall not deliver themselves from the power of the flame: there shall not be a coal to warm at, nor fire to sit before it.*" Astrology is a type of divination that entails forecasting of earthly and human events by the observation and interpretation of the stars. Divination is clearly prohibited by God as we look at Deuteronomy 18:10-12, "*There shall not be found among you anyone that makes his son or his daughter to pass through the fire or that uses divination or an observer of times, or an enchanter or a witch. Or a charmer, or a consulter with familiar spirits or a wizard or a necromancer."* Another conversation I have heard among children is their discussion about playing with a Ouija board. These boards are also known as spirit boards or talking boards. These are also an abomination to the LORD as they are a means to seek answers for future events from evil spiritual beings. A common occurrence in movies is people talking to the dead which is necromancy. Talking to the dead is divination and is an abomination to the LORD, and it can open the door to evil when we engage in these activities. If a child happens to see a movie about necromancy, the child should be told what the Bible says about necromancy. Necromancy which is talking to the dead is a sin according to God's word. We open a dark spiritual door when engaging in these activities. The evil kingdom deceives children, and the demons are spiritual and therefore don't live in this dimension. They operate and monitor us so they know certain things about our life and will use that to trap children into listening to their lies and deceptions.

The words divination and occult refer to the practice of seeking knowledge of the future from other supernatural means other than God. Occult items are dangerous to have in our homes because we are saying that we trust in the occult figure to protect us, not God. Children need to be taught the truth about the occult and divination to protect their imagination from going down this dangerous pathway.

CHAPTER 6
SHINING THE LIGHT ON THE DARKNESS OF VIDEO GAME ADDICTION

In a reading classroom, I was teaching two brothers along with other students. I taught these two brothers for two years. By the time these brothers were in 3rd and 5th grade, they had a very unhealthy connection to video games. During class, they had a hard time not talking about video game characters, video game violence, and their next video game challenge. They even had a video game code language that made it hard to tell what they were talking about. During their season of excessive video game play time, their attitudes towards learning and coming to class drastically changed. They used to have fun and engage with other friends, but now they were disinterested in learning and only wanted to talk about video game topics related to their gaming. The one brother was trying to write a story and all he said he could think about or wanted to write about was violence. I remember when I met these boys and how much progress they made in class but now more recently they were at a standstill because their minds were occupied with the fast pace of video games, the violence of video games, and the witchcraft in many video games. Certain video games, movies, and music contain witchcraft and sorcery that cause addictive behavior. We are not to be ignorant of the devices meant to trap our minds and hold people in bondage to these things.

I have seen a consistent pattern of boy students who lack motivation who also play hours and hours of video games and some of them are obsessed with the games, which ends up leading to an addiction. I talked with a male fifth-grade student about possibly finding something else to do with his time other than video games. I told this student that I noticed he likes to make things with his hands and suggested he spend more time working with his hands to build and create. I gave him a suggestion of taking old things around the house and trying to build something new with them. When my son was about his age, my son attended a summer class where students came together and brought broken toasters, broken fans, broken telephones, etc. and they took them apart to learn how they were put together and made something new from the old parts. This fifth-grade boy had lost his motivation. His imagination had become rusty, and he needed to reengage his creative side. Many boys love building and creating with their hands and the video game industry has grabbed many boys' imaginations and taken them down an unhealthy road. These boys were created for something bigger, and they just need to try out different life skills and experiences to find something they want to use their imagination to create.

I want to share with you a testimony from online, Testimony Share – God Freed Me From Gaming Addiction. This young man said in his written testimony, "*I was stuck in a vicious cycle of playing. The desire to quit got stronger with every passing day, but I was still in bondage to the game. I was suffocating, drowning, and passing away like a withered flower inside of myself. I felt like I was wasting my time on the game, and it was driving me insane. My mom momentarily pulled me out. She couldn't joke about it anymore; she didn't laugh anymore. It seemed she was going insane as well.*" Now let's hear the testimony of how this young man was set free: "*I thought the only way to escape it all was to not live at all. I felt very pushed down. It was until I came across a church still in service. I saw people literally screaming at the top of their lungs at full force. They were not even playing in tune with the musical notes. Some ran as they yelled, so full of energy. I couldn't understand. Why are these people doing this? I could only see one thing…FREEDOM. The freedom that doesn't come from man, but the freedom that comes from God. Jesus tore the chains from me and set me free to live a life full of joy, blessings, and the Holy Spirit. From that day, I lived in freedom.*"

This next testimony is from 2023 written by Melanie Hempe from thegospelcoalition.org, What to do When Your Child is Addicted to Video Games. This testimony is about a boy named Adam addicted to video games and how his mom tried to help him. "*I should have noticed the warning signs in middle school when Adam started dropping out of sports and hobbies to play more* *video games. He also began choosing his gaming world over spending time with us or going to church. I hated my new job as the Game Cop mom, setting the kitchen timer and dealing with constant conflicts over his gaming time. His screen habits grew worse in ninth grade when his school, like many others, issued a laptop to all the students. That was a turning point for our family because we lost all ability to help him manage his screen time. As I walked down the school hall one day to meet the counselor to discuss the problem, I passed a row of boys, all playing <u>Call of Duty</u> on their school-issued laptops. The remainder of Adam's time in high school was filled with conflict—the push and pull of trying to manage life with an unmanageable gaming obsession. I realized we were dealing with something more serious than a bad habit. This had all the signs of an addiction."* Adam's mother was a nurse, and she talked to physicians and neuroscientists to find out that gaming addiction has a neurochemical aspect. *"MRI's show gaming addiction to be neurologically similar to every other addiction. The overproduction of dopamine during games sets off a series of neurochemical events, leading to craving for more. I shifted my thinking in terms of parental limits—like setting curfew or not allowing R-rated movies—to understanding the deeper emotional and spiritual implications of a child lost in the virtual world. Fortunately, our story is filled with redemption. First, nearly 12 years later, Adam is doing well—he served five years in the U.S. Army and graduated college. Now finishing law school, he's also a spokesperson for ScreenStrong the nonprofit organization we started to save kids from the path he took. Adam tells that he wishes he could reclaim the more than 10,000 hours he spent gaming and losing himself in the virtual world."* Furthermore, Adam's mom says, *"The addictive and provocative elements of video games are* *so powerful that I think it's dangerous to allow them into our homes as a valued activity during childhood and then expect our children to thrive. Setting our children up for failure isn't protecting them; it's not wise, and it doesn't honor our Creator."*

Now we will look at an example from a middle school classroom. This boy began to complain about how his mom created all this homework for him to do over the weekend. Later in the same class, this same boy told me how he plays video games the entire weekend. Now it is much clearer why his mom created something useful for his mind to do over the weekend instead of being obsessed with video games. It appears from what I have seen that trying to manage video game use is extremely difficult, especially for those children where video games are now an addiction. It is like putting alcohol in the house and telling the alcoholic to not drink. Some things simply need to be cast out of our lives because of the foothold it has gained in our life.

It was another enlightening day in middle school. The middle school classroom was completing a four-page math handout that contained statistics on the number of hours people played video games by age group. This assignment gave me an open door to ask the students questions about their video game usage. I did a survey of the classes video game usage and about 50% stated they played video games, and they were all boys. Out of the 50% that played video games, 25% played every now and then and the other 25% played approximately 7 hours a day. The entire class seemed very unmotivated to complete this four-page handout;

it took the first 20 minutes of class to find pencils for all the students who didn't have them. I asked the classroom assistant about the class being unmotivated beyond what I had ever seen before, and she said they had noticed that since the students were out of the classroom for so long due to the pandemic that students were just not motivated to achieve their goals in the classroom. I continued asking the students about their video game usage, and two boys told me the reason they were extremely tired in class was because the day before they began an on-line video game marathon at 4:00 pm that lasted until 4:00 am in the morning. These boys got no sleep due to playing video games literally through the night and then got on the bus to come to school. This was how they spent Easter weekend. These two boys needed help being set free from the addiction of on-line video games. They told me that they learn stuff from the video games that help them, but they couldn't really explain to me what that was other than some individuals become rich developing video games and some individuals who are the best players of the game make a lot of money. I tried to plant a seed and tell them that video games don't care about them and that video games are robbing them of their time to grow and learn before becoming an adult. We need to help our children to regain their childlike imaginations for good and not use their imaginations to live in a virtual world that will not help them but will destroy their sense of what is true. The virtual world can not only steal their childhood but steal their future. It is worth fighting for our children and not lowering our standards as to what they are capable of.

It is a wonderful day when a child has revelation and understanding about the power of their choices. In another middle school classroom, a student shared a good decision he made; he stated he decided to join basketball and stop playing World of Warcraft with all his spare time. One simple decision can change the course of a child's life.

CHAPTER 7
THE SEARED CONSCIENCE

What is a seared conscience? Seared means scorched, branded, cauterized, or scalded. A seared conscience has dulled the sense of right and wrong. Therefore, the conscience is not working properly. For example, when an animal has been scarred with a branding iron, that area is numb to further pain.

If someone's conscience is seared, their conscience will actually defend their wrongdoing. A clear conscience or pure conscience will recognize right from wrong. We are born with a conscience where the Law is written in our heart. (Romans 2:15)

Is the child's imagination being drawn into good or evil? According to Philippians 4:8, *"Finally brethren, whatsoever things are true, whatsoever things are honest, whatsoever things are just, whatsoever things are pure, whatsoever things are lovely, whatsoever things are of good report; if there be any virtue, and if there be any praise, think on these things."* This verse gives us a guideline to use to evaluate whether something is virtuous for us to be engaging in. If our conscience becomes seared, our conscience will not be protecting us. Let's look at

Denise White

some examples. If a boy is playing a video game and his goal in the game is to kill characters in the video game, the boy's imagination is thinking on how to eliminate or kill the character in the video game. Now let's use the verse from Philippians 4:8 to evaluate this. Is this activity something true, honest, just, pure, lovely, of good report, virtuous, praiseworthy? Next, if a child is listening to a song where the lyrics are singing about putting spells or curses on someone or if the song lyrics talk about revenge or bitterness, would this be in the category of true, pure, lovely, of good report, virtuous, or praiseworthy? The child's imagination would be thinking about what revenge and bitterness is and maybe even start to imagine in their mind who has caused them pain and if they want to get revenge. Song lyrics can move our imagination in the area of what the lyrics are saying. Life and death are in the power of the tongue. Words do affect children and adults in our imagination. We may start to get angry, depressed, or bitter listening to particular songs. Lastly, if a child is reading a book about sexual seduction, what would the child be imagining? These types of books can sear anyone's conscience as they begin imagining in their minds acts that are not true, not honest, not just, not pure, not lovely, not of good report, not virtuous, and not praiseworthy. This type of reading material can lead the imagination down a road of lust which can lead to acting out in this area. I would imagine that an adult who committed adultery thought about it in their imagination before they actually acted on it. Our imaginations are powerful, and we need to be careful what we are imagining.

Before the plans and purposes are fulfilled in a child's life, they envision them in their imagination. Our imagination is a gift from God to be used for His good purposes. How do we help our children to use their imagination in a God pleasing way? We can help them create, dream, write, draw, paint, build, develop, make things with their hands, encourage their helpfulness, love themselves and others, share, improve something, achieve something, care for and help others, discover something new, to teach someone else, invent, expand on something, enjoy an activity, experience something new, to experiment, enhance something, ponder and consider new opportunities.

How do we heal a seared conscience? The word of God will heal the conscience because it is alive and active. When we speak the word of God aloud and believe it, the power of the Holy Spirit will transform our conscience. The child's conscience and imagination are restored as they think about things that are pure and learn to cast off unpure thoughts.

CHAPTER 8
A SOUND MIND

According to the Merriam Webster dictionary, obsessiveness is excessively often to an unreasonable degree. A synonym for the word obsessive is impulsive. According to the Oxford Languages, compulsiveness results from or relates to an irresistible urge, especially one that is against one's conscious wishes. Synonyms for compulsive are uncontrollable, overpowering, overwhelming, driving, and out of control. We are not talking about personality types, but we are talking about the thoughts and emotions we do not want and those that feel out of our control.

Keep in mind, we are not looking at the clinical side of obsessive-compulsive disorders, but we are looking at the spiritual side of having obsessive thoughts that lead to compulsive behavior. The opposite of obsessiveness is independent, free, calm, and happy. The opposite of compulsive is freedom, liberty, peace, release, and free will. When we are free, peaceful, and joyful, we are living an abundant life. When we are lacking peace, lacking freedom, and lacking independence, we are lacking the life Jesus bought and paid for on the cross.

Denise White

We are going to evaluate what God's word says about a sound mind. Second Timothy 1: 7 says, for God has not given us the spirit of fear (timidity, cowardice); but of power, and of love, and of a sound mind (self-discipline, self-control). We are given free will by God to make decisions in our life. The Holy Spirit does not force His truth on us but gives us free will to study and meditate on His truth to change our lives. Satan's tactics are to force us, push us, drive us, control us, and feed us lies. If we don't understand our choice to reject Satan's lies, we can be trained up in his lies and manipulations over time. This is especially important to teach the child to monitor their thoughts and imagination.

We have control over our thoughts. We have control over what we allow into our minds. Satan and his demons want to entice us into wrong thinking patterns and try to feed us repetitive lies and negative and evil thoughts. For example, we might begin listening to music lyrics that include violence because we love the beat of the song. Now we have been listening to the song for so long that we begin singing the song repeatedly and our conscience has been seared. We aren't consciously aware of what we are saying, but we are speaking death by repeatedly reciting the dark violent lyrics. The song has made some pathways in our mind. Then we begin having dark evil thoughts of violence because of the words fed into our mind over time. The bad habit of listening to violent song lyrics leads to obsessive thoughts of violence and then the person acts out violent behavior.

If this cycle continues, the person may act out repetitive violent acts. This cycle began in the thoughts and that is how it can stop by replacing the dark violent thoughts and feeding the mind with the word of God and what is true, honest, just, pure, lovely, of good report, virtuous, and praiseworthy. We choose what we allow into our minds and Satan wants us to think it is no big deal to watch horror movies, or that it is no big deal to listen to a song artist who writes songs about revenge, or that it is no big deal to listen to a daily podcast from someone speaking from a worldly point of view. Daily thoughts matter. Thought patterns are being formed whether good or bad, whether of truth or lies, whether worldly or Christ-like.

What are some examples of obsessive-compulsive behaviors? Some examples could be obsessive hand washing, obsessively ordering and arranging, hoarding, needing constant reassurance, obsessively checking for locked doors, possibly some eating disorders, unwanted behaviors that you are driven to perform, unwanted thoughts that persist, etc. These are possible examples but could be a whole array of behaviors that are unwanted and excessively over the top from normal behavior.

An important characteristic of obsessive-compulsive behavior is that it is unwanted and intrusive. Obsessive thoughts can cause intense anxiety. The person will have compulsions to repeat certain behaviors that are unreasonable but may cause some relief from obsessive thoughts. The person feels driven to perform the behaviors because of anxiety caused by the obsessive thoughts. A repeated unhealthy thought accepted and meditated on can lead to an emotional response of anxiety, and then lead to the compulsion to act out a particular behavior in hopes of relieving stress, but it is a cycle that continues unless the thoughts are addressed that began the cycle in the first place. Satan loves to cause a problem by giving us dark evil lies to meditate on and then give us a bad solution or bad result (the compulsive behavior). Satan's lies and solutions are always faulty and never bring relief but bondage. But God's answers and solutions are His words of truth that breathe life back into our minds as we meditate on His scriptures. We are spiritual beings who need spiritual truth to flourish and to be set free of the bondage of obsessive thinking and compulsive behavior.

Now I am going to use an example from the classroom and give a hypothesis for the sake of examining how obsessive-compulsive behavior could start. There was a 7th grade boy who wore latex gloves the entire school day. He changed his gloves about four times during the school day. He had a ritual he performed each time he changed his latex gloves. He stayed about four feet away from all the students and teachers as much as possible. Anytime he changed classrooms, the new teacher had to wipe his desk and chair with antibacterial wipes before he would sit down. He walked on his toes and only stepped down on his heels lightly. When he went to the bathroom to wash his hands, he would come back to class soaked in water. I never saw him eat when the other students ate so I am not sure about his eating habits or rituals. His father was in the medical field. Let's hypothesize how the thoughts came into this 7th-grade boy's head and led to his obsessive-compulsive behavior. The boy's father came home and repeatedly talked about germs and viruses and wearing masks and gloves. His father had conversations with his mother about patients and family members getting viruses and their son overheard. The parents kept reminding the boy to wash his hands constantly so he wouldn't get sick. Then the thoughts started coming into the boy's head, "wash your hands, don't touch anybody or anything or you will get germs and get sick." These thoughts kept coming into his head over and over, and the boy didn't know how to process his thoughts or all the conversations about people getting sick from not wearing masks and not wearing gloves. After months of having these intrusive thoughts and overhearing these types of conversations bombarding his mind, the boy began not wanting to touch people or objects. An idea came into his head to wear gloves all the time to avoid having to come in contact with people or objects; this conclusion seemed reasonable at the time but has grown into an unhealthy cycle which has caused him to lose friends and connections with his family. This cycle of obsessive thoughts has resulted in compulsive behavior initially to relieve some stress from the continual thoughts that he doesn't know how to cast down. His wrong thinking patterns have led to a fear of germs 24/7 and have overtaken his life. Everything he does considers the presence of germs and how to avoid them.

How can this boy be set free of these lies and bondage? We are looking at this from a spiritual aspect, not a clinical aspect. God has given me wisdom from His word and that is where I look to for answers to earthly problems. First, the boy needs to discuss his thoughts and emotions with someone he trusts. He needs to be heard and needs to bring the darkness into the light. Satan is the father of lies and therefore lies to our children and tries to convince them they have no choice or no voice and tries to control their emotions by giving them lying thoughts. Some children have been receiving lies from Satan in their heads for years, and they need to start exposing the lies and bring them into the light. Once the boy starts sharing his thoughts, his parents or other trusted adults can explain to him the lies he believes in and how to cast off evil imaginations. This process takes time. Secondly, James 4 says that we are to submit to God, resist the devil, and he will flee. Children need to be taught about their enemy Satan and not be ignorant of his devices like the word of God says. Children need to be taught spiritual principles from God's word to be set free. Simply telling a child to get over it or be positive is not enough. I have witnessed children in schools being told to just be positive, but this was never enough when it was a difficult situation. A 2nd grader had a brother who was just released from the hospital and had attempted suicide. This 2nd grader's brother was now at home after his hospital release and acting out in troublesome ways. This 2nd grader did not have the tools to work through his emotions and the spiritual aspects of what was going on and how to pray. This

2nd grader confided in me and told me he believed in Jesus as his Lord and Savior. I prayed for this boy and told him that God wants to help him and to talk to God about this. After this conversation, the 2nd grader was smiling and got back to his schoolwork. Children need to know that Jesus Christ sets people free from bondage. Jesus Christ died for us to be free and our children to be free. Children need the TRUTH not some sugar coated politically correct words but that when you know the truth, the truth shall make you free.

Now we will continue to look at an article titled "Obsessive-Compulsive Disorders" from https://www.hopkinsmedicine.org/health. The article says: 1.) *"a person with OCD tries to manage these thoughts through rituals"*. 2.) *"Rituals or compulsions are actions that help stop or ease the obsessive thoughts."* 3.) *"Other anxiety problems, depression, eating disorders, or substance use disorder may happen with OCD. Obsessions are unfounded thoughts, fears, or worries. They happen often and cause great anxiety. Reasoning does not help control the obsessions."* Looking at this spiritually, the permanent change comes when we cast down imaginations and every high thing that exalts itself against the knowledge of God, and bringing into captivity every thought to the obedience of Christ.

The second article we will look at is from mayoclinic.org titled "Obsessive-compulsive disorder (OCD)". *"Obsessive-compulsive disorder (OCD) features a pattern of unwanted thoughts and fears (obsessions) that lead you to do repetitive behaviors (compulsions)"*. Additionally,

Denise White

"despite efforts to ignore or get rid of bothersome thoughts or urges, they keep coming back. This leads to more ritualistic behavior – the vicious cycle of (OCD)." Furthermore, *"you may or may not realize that your obsessions and compulsions are excessive or unreasonable, but they take up a great deal of time and interfere with your daily routine and social, school, or work functioning."* Finally, *"engaging in the compulsions brings no pleasure and may offer only a temporary relief from anxiety."* These quotes from mayoclinic.org are obviously from a medical standpoint. Now I will review them from a spiritual standpoint. The word of God says to cast down imaginations and every high thing that exalts itself against the knowledge of God. Therefore, when this article talks about unwanted patterns of thoughts and fears, we are to cast them down. The enemy may bombard us with lying thoughts, but we are responsible for what we do with them. If we have been listening to lying thoughts for a long time, it may be an intense battle to defeat them but with the power of the Holy Spirit, we will win the battle of the mind. Children that may be dealing with these issues need their parents' love and time to talk through what is going on. There are resources available including counseling to help them work through what is going on in their life. It is essential that they get into the word of God, rebuke the lies in their mind, and fill their mind with God's words. When the parent joins together with the child to battle spiritually to regain the child's thought life and imagination, it is a very powerful union. A house divided cannot stand but a house united will stand.

The final article we are looking at is "Why Do Eating Disorders and Obsessive-Compulsive Disorders Co-Occur?" written by Lauren O. Pollack and Kelsie T. Forbush. These authors have published information from a study for the purpose of gaining knowledge about the possible connection between eating disorders and obsessive-compulsive disorders. "*Results suggest that shared personality traits play a key role in the comorbidity between eating disorders characterized by binge eating and dietary restraint and obsessive-compulsive disorder.*" "*Recent research has consistently identified personality traits that are shared between eating disorders and obsessive-compulsive disorders, such as perfectionism and neuroticism.*" How can we look at this spiritually? Are there certain thoughts that someone with an eating disorder may have that are similar thoughts to someone who has developed an obsessive-compulsive disorder? Is it possible that people with these traits have thoughts about their physical flaws and these thoughts are never cast down but ruminated on? For example, Becky wakes up in the morning and the thought comes to her, "Your smile is ugly, your teeth are really crooked, you better not smile". Over time, Becky keeps receiving these thoughts and never telling them to stop but agree with them. Becky keeps receiving thoughts that others are talking about her terrible teeth and ugly smile. Becky stops smiling and starts to withdraw from social activities all based on a lie in her thoughts. Now years later, Becky receives the thought in her mind that she is not only unattractive because of her teeth and smile but now thoughts are coming to her that she is fat and feels out of control of her life. Becky does not know

Denise White

the tactics of Satan and that she is supposed to cast off these thoughts that the demons are putting in her mind. She doesn't know that she is supposed to cast off evil imaginations. Therefore, Becky feels so out of control by these obsessive thoughts that she acts out compulsive behaviors that drastically affect her eating. Before long, she is only eating very few calories a day. The demons will feed lies to children day after day, month after month, year after year, and if children are not taught to cast off these evil imaginations, the tactics of Satan can lead to destruction in their lives.

But there is hope, peace, joy, love, and breakthrough through Jesus Christ. We can all pray for those in need that they will come to the knowledge of the truth. We can all read our Bible and have our spiritual ammunition ready and our faith shield up to extinguish all the flaming darts of the evil one. The sound mind comes from speaking the life-giving word of God out of your mouth until revelation comes and you actually believe what you are saying. For as he thinks in his heart, so is he! (Proverbs 23:7)

CHAPTER 9
RENEWING THE CHILD'S MIND

The video game Minecraft is quite present in the life of the youth of today. I thought the game was called Mindcraft. I knew little about this game except children told me it was a video game about creating a world with Legos which seemed relatively harmless. Quite a few 6- and 7-year-olds talk about Minecraft at school. I researched what is within the Minecraft video game world. Minecraft has a goal to survive where players obtain resources to build their world and maintain health. There is a kill command in this game. You can become strong and invincible in the game. To regain your health in the game, you either eat food or drink potions. You can also brew potions in the game. The game also contains witches and zombies that spawn in the dark. There was more to this game than I ever thought.

Very young students have been playing a game on the playground where they try to kill each other and even scratch each other while playing. This game was stopped right away, and they said they were playing a Minecraft game. This particular group of students play Minecraft at home. I even had to stop them from writing on their classroom assignments with what they called "Minecraft" writing. One student started writing in this Minecraft writing and three others followed. The child's imagination is powerful and what they do with their imagination matters. When they play this video game, they are using their imagination to create a world and then they act it out on the playground.

I believe the video game world that is targeting the younger child is leading them into more intense violent video games as they become teenagers because once they conquer a game or it becomes boring, they move to another thing to conquer. Minecraft might seem innocent but if you sit down with your child and play with them, you might actually find out more than you bargained for.

The mind of a child is still growing, and video games have a strong impact on the pathways of their minds. They can become unmotivated and obsessed with living in a virtual world where they can control and conquer. They may even start to identify more in a virtual world than in the real world. They may start to identify as gamer and their true identity in Christ is lost. What can we do to help our children?

The mind is one of the most powerful resources a child has and when we teach them how to renew their mind, we are giving them tools for a lifetime. Leading our children to use their imagination in a healthy way and helping them find out who they are and what they were made to be is directing them into their destiny. Life in Christ is not boring but adventurous and exciting as children explore their own creativity. As followers of Christ and parents, we are not to teach our children to conform to the patterns of this world but to guide them into all truth in scripture to transform the child's mind so our little ones can determine what is good and acceptable to God for their lives.

Fear and anxiety are very present in many children's lives. Fear and anxiety can block the child from processing information. I had a fourth-grade student who was struggling with her first-grade sight words and seemed to be struggling with this entire workbook assignment. She was attempting to read words in her reading grade level. I had about twenty minutes of quality time with her. I noticed her body was tense, and she looked afraid. Then suddenly, she started to cry, and I had compassion for her and got her tissues and talked with her. She told me her memory is poor, and she practices these sight words often but can't remember them. I talked with her about how fear and anxiety can cause tension in her body and can prevent her mind from working efficiently. I had her practice releasing tension out of her belly and told her to repeat aloud "I can do it". After about five minutes of discussing these things with her, she began to realize she does have choices that will help her memory. She became happy and was smiling and began practicing and remembering her sight words. I could see the tension in her face and body language before and then the difference after we discussed her choices. It was a good thing that day for her to recognize the actions and thoughts that she was experiencing that were not helping her but hurting her. I could see on her face that fear and anxiety were blocking her ability to think and remember. In addition, I discussed with her the choice to speak aloud, "I can do this" is beginning to shut down the lies in her head that are telling her she can't do it. This young girl seemed to return to believing in her ability to move forward in learning and have hope again. Another thing I have noticed in large classrooms is that sometimes the quiet ones may not ask for help but really need it. That day I was given a great opportunity to speak life to this young girl; sometimes all a child may need is someone who has time to invest in them. Later she came up to me and asked me how to spell my name because she was writing me out a Valentine card since it was Valentine's Day! This little girl went from believing she was defeated to becoming an overcomer. Her mind was renewed little by little that day.

CHAPTER 10
PROTECTING THE CHILD'S SENSES AND THEIR SOUL

There are gates (openings) to our physical body and gates (openings) to our soul. Our senses are the gates to our physical body; ear gates, eye gates, nose gates, skin gates, and mouth gate (taste). Our soul gates (openings) are our heart and mind. If children watch a horror movie, evil can access the child through their eyes. I have seen this from a child at school who had psychological problems and talked to me about various horror movies he was allowed to watch at home, and the child knew it affected him. We are also told in scripture to guard our hearts. We need to guard our hearts and not allow lies and hurts to damage or fracture our soul. Therefore, it is important the parents guard the child and watch out for who is getting close to their children.

We also need to protect the gate to our children's soul. Children can have unhealthy soul ties to others. For example, children playing on-line video games that are occult, violent, or some other evil, can have soul ties to another video game player at the other end. These virtual relationships are built where gamers, who we really don't know, can have demonic influence in their life and the player on the other end can become oppressed with that demonic influence. Demonic influence from one person can pass through to the other person when they are in a relationship (having a soul connection). The spiritual realm is real and there are manifestations in the physical world that originated in the spiritual realm from activities participated in.

Furthermore, the mind needs to be protected. The word of God tells us to cast off evil thoughts and imaginations. Children need to be taught how to protect their mind and to cast off evil thoughts and imaginations. Fear is a common root problem for some children, and if they don't understand what the word of God says about fear, they won't know how to handle this. For God has not given us a spirit of fear; but of power, and of love, and of a sound mind. Fear is an evil spirit. How do you remove fear? According to 1 John 4:18, *"There is no fear in love; but perfect love casts out fear, because fear has torment. He that fears is not made perfect in love."* I have seen children who have anxiety, which is a form of fear, have a harder time retaining information because fear and anxiety are taking up space in the brain where processing occurs. This child is not living their best life.

I was working in a small special needs classroom with two amazingly caring and kind paraprofessionals. There were only four students in this class. All four of the students had trouble handling their emotions. There was a small room for the students to go to when they felt like their emotions were out of their control. Two of the students became very angry throughout the day. These two students were discussing during the day that they both played World of Warcraft. One boy said his favorite movie was Alien vs. Predator. These boys were first-grade students, probably six or seven years of age. The things we expose to our eye gates and ear gates affect us. Especially when children are young and being exposed to things that their emotions and spirits are quite sensitive to.

I had a conversation with one of my students who was struggling. He said he watches shows that make him angry and scared. After our discussion, he seemed to agree with me that he should not watch shows or play video games with violence because it is causing him to manifest anger and fear. Sometimes these things are common sense; if we are manifesting behaviors of anger and fear, we need to eliminate the cause of the torment not just keep doing the same thing and expect a different outcome. This boy knew the cause of his torment; he just needed someone to talk it through with him and then take action to make a change.

Another incredible child I was blessed to meet was a young boy. We built a relationship over three years. He had a serious childhood illness that he had partly recovered from. He was an extremely sensitive boy who was very aware of other people's needs. He had some unusual family dynamics, and I had become aware of the strained relationship between his mother and his father who were now divorced and both dating other people. There was some bitterness going on between family members that I witnessed. This boy was always trying to make other people happy. I prayed for this boy and over his mind since he struggled with memory problems. This boy was very bright and very aware and sensitive to emotional stress. By talking to our children and having deep and meaningful conversations, we can find out what is going on in their minds and hearts and help protect their gates. As their parents, we need to be their gatekeepers and pray for protection over their eye gates, ear gates, nose gates, skin gates, mouth gate, and their minds and hearts. But we need to most importantly, close the gates where Satan is accessing the children!

CHAPTER 11
TESTING THE SOURCE

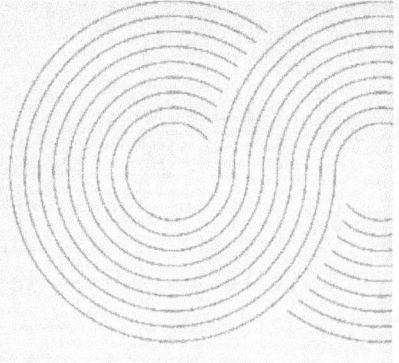

What is the source of what we are doing or using? Who made the product we are buying? When we are consuming products, do we know who created the movie, designed the clothing, wrote the song, and created the video game, book, or website? What are we absorbing from someone else's creation? Is the person a Satan worshipper who is designing the clothing line you buy and wear? Is the song artist you listen to writing lyrics about violence, sex, hatred, revenge, etc.?

One aspect of protecting yourself and your children from evil is to test the source of something. This is a part of wisdom and discernment to evaluate and test the source of what you are watching, what you are listening to, what activity you are engaging in, what relationships you are in, etc.

Let's look at practical examples of testing the source. If you are looking for a new job, research what the company stands for. If you are deciding what school your child will go to, research who started the school and what their beliefs are. If you are thinking about joining a group, find out about the group leader and their belief system. If you are going to buy a new book, investigate the author and if they teach about ungodly topics, such as occult activities, which are quite common today. If you have met a new friend, before you invest too much time into this friendship, ask the new friend deep questions where you can determine what they believe and how they live their lives. If your child is going to a new school, try to visit the school and specifically the child's classroom to see what kind of objects the teacher has in her classroom and meet with the teacher. Research the parents of your child's friends to see if their belief system lines up with yours. Most often it is easy to find out about people, groups, and organizations just by spending some time investigating. Also, it is really important to listen to your instincts and don't ignore what could be plainly in sight. We are to test the spirit behind people, organizations, schools, etc. The world system is to just accept anything and everything, but we know this is the biggest deception. God says not to be ignorant of the enemy's devices.

My testimony of testing the source was when I went on a job interview. I have always wanted to be a Children's Ministry Director where I could teach children how to cast off evil imaginations, teach them the biblical principles of the Bible to live their life by, and teach them Mark 16:15-20. Not long ago, I went to two job interviews at a church for a Children's Ministry Director. One Pastor said they were looking for someone who could draw and keep children interested and having fun. It didn't seem my style since I am bold for the cause of Christ, and it seemed more like selling parents and children on how entertaining the programs could be. Another interview I went on was shocking how things developed as we talked. The Pastor and I had a great conversation and then after about 30 minutes he asked a question that revealed a lot, *"if you were having a conversation with someone in our church that lives the gay lifestyle, would you be accepting of their beliefs?"* I spoke from the heart and answered from a scripture perspective and ended up talking about what the Bible had to say about this topic. The Pastor was very interested in our conversation, and I felt it was a ministry moment where God gave me an opportunity to speak the truth. This was no longer a job interview but a time for me to speak the truth into this Pastor's life, and I left feeling we both had a lot to process about what just happened during this job interview. It gave me an opportunity to be tested as to what would come out of my mouth when asked this question. The whole conversation from both the Pastor's side and mine was all done with kindness and love but truthful. We parted ways and both knew we saw things completely differently. However, I felt that the Pastor was truly processing our discussion even though it seemed he would continue business as usual. Something extremely bothersome about this interview was the plans of that church to have a children's program that draws children in by having fun activities but isn't biblically sound. Satan will try to slip things into our children's lives. This is why testing the source is vital today and just as important is parent involvement because it is hard to hide things from a parent who is actively involved in their child's activities and life.

Another testimony of testing the source was when I moved to a new town and was looking for a church. My husband and I were going to go to church to celebrate the resurrection of Jesus Christ and were planning to go to this specific church. This was a non-denominational Christian church which was throughout the United States. I wanted to research this church and went online and found two articles written by local people warning others of the cult-like characteristics of this church. A gentleman who gave a very large amount to the church began asking where the money was used, and the church began to try to quiet him and would not answer him. Also, I was working at a school, and a coworker told me that she visited this same church and found it was cult-like. She went a few times to the church and the last time she was there; she wasn't allowed to leave when she wanted to. They were trying to use verbal force to keep her there. She had to use force of her own to threaten them to let her go. She never returned. Common sense tells us something is wrong with this. My husband and I never went to the church.

It is important to teach our children how to test the source of things and use their discernment. For example, if your child is insisting on watching a television show, investigate with them the theme of the story or who created the television show. Another example is if they want to play a video game and you know nothing about it, investigate with them the theme of the video game and the creator. It is important that children learn to use their discernment to make wise decisions for their lives. Teaching them to listen to the Holy Spirit and study the word of God is necessary so they know what God wants them to be doing with their time. If we teach our children to investigate for themselves what a movie is about or even what a potential friend believes before making a friendship, these are priceless teaching moments. Teaching children to be discerning and to listen to their conscience is a gift to them for their lifetime. If you are watching a movie with your child and it contains some questionable aspects, discuss this with them if they are old enough to have a conversation about the topic. There are many children's movies, supposedly innocent, full of occult and dark spiritual aspects that can be very confusing and dangerous to a child. If we use this opportunity to explain what God says in scripture about not connecting ourselves to occult things and explain why they will not be allowed to watch this movie, it will hopefully help them take ownership of discerning what is right or wrong, good or bad for themselves. Using these opportunities to build their knowledge about the word of God and helping them not to be ignorant of Satan's devices is priceless knowledge. If the source of a movie is occult-related, we should not be watching, and of course neither should our children. They will observe what we watch so we need to be consistent with this message of staying away from occult movies or objects.

Denise White

When we are testing the source, we are actually testing the spirit behind it. Is it of the spirit of light or the spirit of darkness? A short time ago, I was listening to an audio of the Bible and was led to investigate the source of who posted the Bible audio. After about 15 minutes of investigating, I was shocked to find what the author of the YouTube channel believed. Their website stated plainly that he (the man who created the YouTube channel) believed he was Jesus Christ. The pictures on his website were very strange. After my investigation into the source of this Bible audio YouTube channel, I immediately stopped listening to this Bible audio YouTube channel. I was joyful that the Holy Spirit led me to recognize this false teacher. We must be aware of the source of what we listen to, what we watch, and who we associate with, etc. Satan and his evil minions know the scripture too!! This false teacher could have spoken curses, added words, or deleted scripture over the medium he puts out; therefore, after I recognized the true source of his audio, I prayed over my mind and heart. Beware of the Deceiver and his evil workers. Furthermore, I was listening to a preacher of truth on a radio station, and he was discussing how he sees a lot of Christians listening to popular radio and podcast commentators who are very wise and have great common sense but don't believe Jesus Christ is Lord. Basically, the pastor was saying how this can be dangerous if we are listening to the thoughts of these popular and famous radio commentators who have no belief in the Lord Jesus Christ, and they feed you with the knowledge of the world without any truths from the Word of God.

Over time, our minds can soak up a lot of worldly knowledge that creates a stronghold in our thinking.

It is important we know the source of what our children are being taught and what their teacher believes. This not only applies to the elementary, middle school, and high school classrooms but also applies to college instructors because what the college and the college professors believe will infiltrate into the college classroom as well. The teacher's beliefs will infiltrate the classroom whether good or bad. Even more important is the belief system of the school and principal. I was frequently working at an elementary school, and whenever I worked there, it was such a pleasure because of the atmosphere of leadership, order, and support. The principal was very visible in the school and had great communication with the students and staff. When I worked there for a weeklong job, the principal told me I was a blessing and told me if I needed anything, he would get it for me. As we had a casual discussion, I could see he was a man of faith, and this school was quite orderly because of the source at the top.

Testing the source of where something originated, is a way to determine if something is of God or Satan. We are not to be ignorant of Satan's devices. Therefore, we want to have some knowledge of the traps Satan tries to lure our children into. One of these traps is the dangerous fascination with vampires. First, let us look at the definition of a vampire from Oxford Languages: 1.) A corpse supposed in European folklore, to leave its grace at night to drink the blood of the living by biting their necks with long pointed canine teeth. Merriam-Webster's definition: 1.) the reanimated body of a dead person believed to come from the grave at night and suck the blood of persons asleep. 2.) one who lives by preying on others, 3.) a woman who exploits and ruins her lover; and 4.) a vampire bat. None of those definitions are something we want to be associated with. Defining a word is a good starting point for understanding the source of something. Back in 2005, there was a very popular vampire series that began, and a lot of young Christians and many others were big fans of it. But let's assess the source of this series. According to an article "The Darkness of Twilight" written by Sue Bohlin on June 27, 2010, on Bible.org; the author of the Twilight series had a dream that gave her the idea for this series. Her dream was of two people falling in love and one of them was a "fantastically beautiful, sparkly, and a vampire". Think about this; Satan himself masquerades as an angel of light.

Let's take a closer look at the "Twilight" series. It is based on a girl in a relationship with a vampire, and the story is full of lustful obsession. A quote from Sue's article, *"But all forms of entertainment are a wrapper for values and a message, and we need to be aware of what it is. Remember, what we take into our imaginations is really like food for our souls. If something has poison in it, it shouldn't be eaten."* If you have a child drawn to this type of entertainment, I suggest you pull the full article written by Sue Bohlin on "The Darkness of Twilight" to help you understand all the dark aspects of this series so you can have the information you need to fight this spiritual battle.

Furthermore, I want to review what the Bible says about blood and this topic:

1) *"Only be sure that thou eat not the blood: for the blood is the life; and thou mayest not eat the life with the flesh."* (Deuteronomy 12:23)
2) *"And whatsoever man there be of the house of Israel or of the strangers that sojourn among you, that eateth any manner of blood; I will even set my face against that soul that eateth blood, and will cut him off from among his people. For the life of the flesh is in the blood: and I have given it to you maketh an atonement for the soul."* (Leviticus 17:10-11)
3) *"Moreover ye shall eat no manner of blood, whether it be of fowl or of beast, in any of your dwellings. Whatsoever soul it be that eateth any manner of blood, even that soul shall be cut off from his people."* (Leviticus 7:26-27)
4) *"For it seemed good to the Holy Spirit and to us, to lay upon you no greater burden than these necessary things; that ye abstain from meats offered idols, and from blood, and from things strangled, and from fornication: from which if ye keep yourselves, ye shall do well. Farewell"* (Acts 15:28-29)

Therefore, being entertained by reading books or watching movies where they hunt and drink blood, is evil at its source and dangerous to our souls. Testing the source of things we allow into our mind, heart,

Denise White

body, home, and life is not a waste of time but invaluable to ourselves and our children.

CHAPTER 12

STANDING GUARD FOR THE CHILDREN

We are to stand guard for our children. One area where we need to stand guard for our children is the airwaves. The airwaves are the body of communication in the air such as radio, television, cell phones, social media airwaves, online gaming, etc. Ephesians 2:2 says, *"Wherein in time past you walked according to the course of this world, according to the prince of the power of the air, the spirit that now worketh in the children of disobedience."* Satan is the prince of the power of the air. Therefore, Satan's power is in the airwaves, and he moves his agenda and plans through the airwaves. Furthermore, we do not wrestle with people but against spiritual wickedness.

Now let's examine some examples of standing guard for the children. It was Aurora's birthday, and she came to her third-grade class all dressed up in a lovely princess dress and a birthday button attached to her dress letting everyone know it was her birthday. She brought everyone in her class a bag of treats and toys. It was late morning, and she came to me crushed in spirit and in tears. She said a student walked past her in the hallway and said to her, "I hope you have the worst birthday!" What could I do to help this little girl? The students started talking about being kind to one another, so I used this opportunity to help Aurora. I asked the class that whoever had words of kindness to speak to Aurora on her birthday to raise their hand. Then one at a time, the students told Aurora special things about herself. By the time this was over, Aurora's spirit was lifted and hopefully those words spoken to her in the hallway were squashed. The students helped Aurora get her imagination off of what the student said in the hallway to her and now she was imagining and meditating on the kind words of her classmates.

I was a guest teacher in a 2nd-grade classroom. I met an amazing 2nd grade boy who wore blue jeans, a long-sleeved button-down shirt, and a cowboy hat that appeared to be worn often. He brought in spurs that his uncle made for show and tell. He told me his grandpa has a horse and cattle farm. He told me he is a good cowboy and better at roping than his dad or grandpa. On this same school day, the lesson plan was to discuss different emotions with the children and read a book related to this topic. The book I was given to read to the children confused them and me. The book seemed to imply that we are enough within ourselves and gave no place for God. I used this as an opportunity to talk about their feelings and what was going on in their mind and heart. As we continued to discuss emotions, this other 2nd grade student was saying how his emotions are most often bland with no happiness or sadness but just unemotional. He also shared he is more often sad than happy. When he was done sharing, I asked him if he had faith in the LORD, and he said he did. I told him to pray and ask the Lord for joy. He seemed to agree and went on his way. When children know and have discovered something about themselves that is unique to them, like this 2nd grader who was a cowboy, they seem much happier. It is a battle worthy of our time and attention to help children find the special attributes about them and how God made them unique. The wonderful teacher of this class called her children "sweethearts" throughout the day and the day I was there, they reminded me to call them "sweethearts" and it warmed my heart.

In this same classroom, there was a 2nd grade girl with an autoimmune disease and another girl with a severe eczema problem. The girl with the eczema problem mentioned briefly she has some trouble at home. I only get a glimpse into these children's lives but what I have learned over my years of studying God's word and learning from healing and deliverance ministries, is that we need to look at the heart of the children and ask them what is going on in their lives and work through their heartaches, pains, disappointments, etc. with them to help them move into their abundant life.

Today I was the guest teacher in a third-grade class. As I went out to get my class from recess, the recess attendant was telling me about Becca and how Becca was saying she couldn't remember anything.

Denise White

The recess attendant was suspicious of Becca's story. Becca said she hit her head and couldn't remember her name or what happened earlier, but there was no incident where she hit her head at recess. I watched Becca closely as we went back to class. I discovered a very strange relationship between Becca and this other girl in the class named Isabel. Isabel was treating Becca like a baby and enabling this student. Isabel kept going over to Becca and saying, "are you okay?" "Do you know your name?" "I can help you and watch out for you?" Isabel was telling me that Becca couldn't do her work because she couldn't remember anything. But I heard Becca talking to others and seemed fine. I talked to Isabel and told her that her fellow student is not a baby, and that Isabel is responsible for her work and herself and not for Becca. Becca is responsible for Becca and if she is telling a lie or you are telling a lie you are responsible for your actions. Shortly after this, I moved Isabel away from Becca's chair and both students worked hard for the remainder of the day. This strange relationship that was forming between these students was very unhealthy, and it was evident that it was causing them to have an unhealthy relationship that fed into their insecurities. Once both students were confronted separately and they saw their lies were exposed, they knew their behavior was wrong. The students continued the rest of the day working, and there was no more talk about this nonsense. Children are amazing in how quickly they let things go and receive the truth.

As we stand guard over our children to protect them from the wiles of the enemy, we can declare life giving words over their mind, body, soul, and spirit. Praying scripture over our children is powerful as we believe in faith the words we declare. The following are just some examples of scriptures you can pray over your children:

- For God has not given (child's name) the spirit of fear; but of power, and of love, and of a sound mind. (2 Timothy 1:7)
- For I know the thoughts that I think toward (child's name), says the LORD, thoughts of peace and not of evil, to give you a future and a hope. (Jeremiah 29:11)
- (Child's name) shall not die, but live, and declare the works of the LORD. (Psalm 118:17)

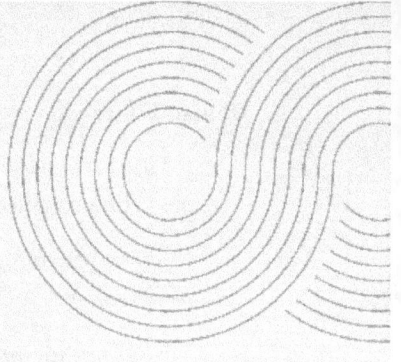

CHAPTER 13

NOT LOWERING OUR STANDARDS FOR OUR CHILDREN

What are the standards for teaching children? What does the word of God teach us about bringing up children in the LORD?

"Train a child in the way he should go; and when he is old, he will not depart from it." (Proverbs 22:6)

"And, you fathers, provoke not your children to wrath; but bring them up in the nurture and admonition of the Lord." (Ephesians 6:4)

"The rod and reproof give wisdom: but a child left to himself brings his mother to shame." (Proverbs 29:15)

"He that spares his rod hates his son: but he that loves him chastens him diligently." (Proverbs 13:24)

"And these words, which I command you this day, shall be in your heart: and you shall teach them diligently to your children, and shall talk of them when you sit in your house, and when you walk by

the way, and when you lie down, and when you rise up." (Deuteronomy 6:7)

"Fathers provoke not your children to anger, lest they be discouraged." (Colossians 3:21)

"Withhold not correction from the child: for if you beat him with the rod, he shall not die. You shall beat him with the rod and shall deliver his soul from hell." (Proverbs 23:13-14)

"Correct your son, and he shall give you rest; yea, he shall give delight to your soul." (Proverbs 29:17)

"Foolishness is bound in the heart of a child; but the rod of correction shall drive it far from him." (Proverbs 22:15)

"But Jesus said, Permit little children, and forbid them not, to come to Me: for of such is the kingdom of heaven. And He laid His hands on them, and departed from there." (Matthew 19:14-15)

"And all your children shall be taught of the LORD; and great shall be the peace of your children." (Isaiah 54:13)

"But if any provide not for his own, and especially for those of his own house (family), he has denied the faith, and is worse than an infidel (unbeliever)." (1 Timothy 5:8)

"I have no greater joy than to hear that my children walk in truth." (3 John 4)

"And that from a child you have known the holy scripture, which are able to make you wise to

salvation through faith which is in Christ Jesus. All scripture is given by inspiration of God, and is profitable for doctrine (teaching), for reproof, for correction, for instruction in righteousness." (2 Timothy 3:15-16)

"Before I formed you in the womb, I knew you; before you were born I sanctified you; I ordained you a prophet to the nations." (Jeremiah 1:5)

Two of the above verses speak to fathers and warn against provoking their children to anger. To provoke is to stir up, to excite, and to call forth. Parents are to stir up good in their children and not say or do things that the parent knows will agitate or anger but speak truth in love.

Furthermore, four of these verses talk about disciplining our children, Proverbs 23 powerfully says the rod of correction shall deliver a soul from hell. We are not to withhold discipline from our children. The Bible teaches children about the fear of the LORD and to honor their mother and father. Some children may listen to their parents without much scolding, but others may be rebellious and need stricter discipline. If we simply look at the world and the rebellious nature of the world, we can see what happens when we look at God's word as only a suggestion. But God's word is to protect us from harm. God is a loving Father who knows some children need stricter discipline than others. We are to always be wise in handling the discipline of our children, but we are not to eliminate firm discipline because some children may require repeated reminders for them to turn from their rebellious ways. Some children adjust their behavior after being disciplined the first time, but other children may need follow-up reminders.

As we look at the above verse in Jeremiah, we read about the importance of a child knowing their identity. Each child was born with a purpose and a plan for their life, and it is important for the child to know that God made them unique and special with a purpose and hope. A child that knows that their father and mother love them, and they have a loving relationship with them is much more likely to want to please their parents. The same applies to wanting to please our Heavenly Father. When we know how much our Heavenly Father loves us and that His discipline is to save our souls, we want to follow His biblical principles for our good.

We are not to conform to the patterns or standards of this world. This world keeps lowering its standards of what is acceptable. Therefore, if the standards are also lowered for children, children will most likely only live up to the lower standard set. The farther families and schools move away from the standards set by God (in His commands and principles of the Bible), the lower the standards the children are expected to live up to. A major issue I have personally witnessed and been on the other end of is the lack of respect for authority and even challenging and debating with the authority. I also have seen children intentionally try to drive a teacher into saying something that will give them cause against the teacher. I have had students yell out "black lives matter" randomly to get a reaction. I have witnessed students speak loudly back and forth saying "Are you questioning my gender identity?" I also hear it said frequently back and forth between students "You're racist". Children know the trigger points and what is going on in society. There is a lot of fear out there with these sensitive topics, but for the Christian household, these issues should be talked about. When society keeps lowering the standard, the Christian household must grow stronger in the word of God. What standards does God say we are to live by? First and foremost, we are to love the Lord our God with all our heart, soul, mind, and strength. Secondly, we are to love our neighbors as ourselves. Therefore, children are to love God, themselves, and others. Loving others does not mean agreeing with their beliefs; it means loving them and lovingly speaking the truth when prompted by the Holy Spirit. Additionally, the Bible is full of biblical principles to live by which is why it is important to teach our children these truths in scripture. The children need to know what God's standard is and that we are accountable to God for our actions. The confusion of the world brings confusion to children and the more we can teach our children God's standards, the more it will bring order to their minds and hearts. *"And be not conformed to this world: but be you transformed by the renewing of your mind, that you may prove what is that good, and acceptable, and perfect, will of God."* (Romans 12:2)

If someone has a seared conscience, their conscience has been dulled, and therefore the safeguard to make them aware of evil is no longer present. When I substitute teach in high school classrooms, it is most likely that I will hear the "f" word spoken frequently. As a substitute teacher I have authority over that classroom for that day, but what I have noticed is if I try to eliminate a bad behavior in a day it usually backlashes. It is like poking a monster; it just makes it worse. But what I have observed is when the school unites and agrees on a disciplinary plan and rules that every classroom follows, there is a great change. One high school I was teaching in had very little cursing and swearing in the classroom and this school had good unity and common rules amongst the classrooms regarding profanity. Their policies did not lower their expectations of the student's ability to comply with certain behavior; they seemed to expect improvement and set standards in place to help the students set goals to improve behavior and not view poor behavior as commonplace and acceptable. I want to look a little further into why the "f" word is used and overused by young people. It is the most common profanity that I hear. According to the Oxford Language it means: 1) have sex with someone, 2) ruin or damage something. According to the Merriam Webster dictionary it can additionally mean: to deal with unfairly or harshly. Merriam Webster also indicates it is a word used to display obscenity or vulgarity. The urban dictionary additionally indicates it is used as an exaggeration by placing the word before another they would like to further express. Why has this word become so common among our youth? Is it possible they don't feel heard and have found a way to emphasize what they are saying so someone will listen. Let's see what God's word says about our spoken words.

1) We are to edify and bless others. Our profane words affect ourselves and others and our ignorance, to that, hurts ourselves and others. Ephesians 4:29 says, *"Let no corrupt communication proceed out of your mouth, but that which is good to the use of edifying, that it may minister grace unto the hearers."*

2) We will give an account to God of every careless word we spoke. Matthew 12:36-37 says, *"But I say unto you, That every idle word that men shall speak, they shall give account thereof in the day of judgment. For by thy words thou shalt be justified, and by thy words thou shall be condemned."*

3) Our words are producing death or life! Proverbs 18:21, *"Death and life are in the power of the tongue: and they that love it shall eat the fruit thereof."*

One of the definitions of the "f" word was to "ruin or damage". What intention of our heart do we have when we are speaking this word and what are we producing? Have we lowered our expectations of children and no longer bring to their attention their cursing or swearing because everybody else does it too? In addition, this word seems to be a sign of rebellion. Children know they get a reaction when they use it, and their peers generally expect them to use it to fit in.

If we lower our standards and say, "Well, all the other teenagers swear and say inappropriate words all the time, and since our son only says the "f" word occasionally it isn't so bad." Ignoring or simply not addressing our children's wrong behavior may avoid present arguments, but in the long run, it will catch up with us. Later the slippery slope comes into play, and they have moved into other wrong behaviors like increased cursing and swearing, fornication, lying, stealing, etc. God's word needs to be our standard because if we determine the standard depending on what other parents are doing or what we think, this will only lead to continually lowering the standard of what is acceptable and then allowing sin into our home and accepting it as okay when it is not okay with God.

I want to celebrate those teachers who love their students and speak life over them. I was teaching in a first-grade classroom, and the students told me to call them "little darlings" because that is what their teacher calls them. That is precious! In some other classrooms, teachers have encouraging scripture verses hung on their computer or desk area to encourage them. There are specific schools and classrooms where the level of respect is great. I have noticed in most of the classrooms where there is a great level of respect that it usually begins at the top. These schools usually have inspirational messages from the principal at the beginning of the day which set the standard for the day. The schools that continue to require students to stand for the pledge of allegiance are another sign of respect in the school and classroom. I have been in some middle school classes and some high school classes where not all students stand for the pledge. Also, the schools that require students to remove hats and hoodies in the classroom have greater respect in the classroom. The lower we set our standards, the lower we meet the standard.

It is important that I set a standard for myself and set a standard in the classroom. There were two instances in different classrooms where students went down on one knee and bowed in front of me. In one classroom, there was a boy on each side of me that bowed down. I said, "Why are you doing that?" And there was no answer from either of them. Shortly before this happened, they were both laughing in class, and it was of a mocking nature; it sounded demonic. I had gone over to them and spoken to them about their behavior and that it needed to stop. I recently listened to a video of a deliverance Pastor saying that the enemy must bow to the servant of the Lord Jesus Christ. When I teach in the classroom, I use the authority I have through my faith in Jesus Christ to take authority over my classroom. I am working as a servant of the LORD in the classroom to set the captive free, and I can't lower my standard. When we become a new creation in Christ and the old man is drowned out, we are at a new standard. When we know better, we must do better by the strength of the kingdom of God living inside of us. This is the new standard for a believing child.

CHAPTER 14:

TEACHING CHILDREN THE TRUTH

I was watching a movie on YOUTUBE about a young boy who believed in Jesus and His miracle healing power, but both of His parents didn't understand why their son was so interested in Jesus and reading about Him in the Bible. This boy used to read comics but gave that up to read the Bible. Children are very curious, and this boy was very curious to learn about Jesus and nothing else compared to his interest in Jesus. His faith was contagious and others around him were drawn to the Lord as he professed his faith and testified of miracles that happened. When we put truth in the children's hands, it is quite powerful. We are told by the LORD to bring the children to Him and not to hinder the little children.

Truths to teach our children:

A.) Honoring our father and our mother is a command from God. When we dishonor our parents, we disobey the LORD. Let's see what the word of God says about this. Exodus 21:17 says, *"And he that curseth his father, or his mother, shall surely be put to death."* Matthew 15:4, *"For*

Denise White

God commandeth, saying, Honor thy father and mother: and He that curseth father or mother, let him die the death." Deuteronomy 27:16, *'Cursed is he who dishonors (treats with contempt) his father and his mother.' And all the people shall say, 'Amen'.* Exodus 20:12, *"Honor thy father and thy mother: that thy days may be long upon the land which the LORD thy God giveth thee."* Ephesians 6:2-3, *"Honor thy father and mother; which is the first commandment with promise. That it may be well with thee, and thou mayest live long on the earth."* Proverbs 20:20, *"Whoso curseth his father or his mother, his lamp shall be put out in obscure darkness."* Proverbs 30:17, *"The eye that mocks his father, and scorns his mother, the ravens of the valley shall pick it out, and the young vultures will devour it."* Proverbs 19:26, *"He who mistreats his father and chases away his mother is a son that causes shame and brings reproach."* Exodus 21:17, *"And he that curses his father, or his mother, shall surely be put to death."* Exodus 21:15, *"And he that strikes his father, or his mother, shall be surely put to death."* God's word isn't vague or unclear but explains itself clearly for the children to understand the order He has created.

B.) <u>Forgiving ourselves and others</u>; *"For if you forgive men their trespasses, your Heavenly Father will also forgive you: but if you forgive not men their trespasses, neither will your Father forgive your trespasses."*

C.) <u>Do not be offended</u>; *"These things have I spoken unto you, that you should not be offended."* (John 16:1). *"The discretion of a man makes him slow to anger; and his glory is to overlook a transgression."* (Proverbs 19:11)

D.) <u>Be content with what you have</u>; *"Let your conversation be without covetousness; and be content with such things as you have: for he hath said, I will never leave thee, nor forsake thee."* (Hebrews 13:5)

E.) <u>Deny ungodliness and worldly lusts</u>; *"Teaching us that denying ungodliness and worldly lusts, we should live soberly, righteously, and godly, in this present world."* (Titus 2:12)

F.) <u>Be careful who your friends are</u>; *"And have no fellowship with the unfruitful works of darkness, but rather reprove them."* (Ephesians 5:11)

G.) <u>Cast off evil imaginations</u>; 1 Corinthians 2:16, Romans 12:2, Isaiah 26:3, Colossians 3:1-2, Philippians 4:4-9, 2 Corinthians 10:3-6, 1 Peter 1:13.

We are told in 2 Corinthians 10:5, *"Casting down imaginations, and every high thing that exalts itself against the knowledge of God and bringing into captivity every thought to the obedience of Christ."*

It is essential that our children be taught to recognize thoughts, imaginations, and dreams that are evil and against God's word. If children are having bad dreams or nightmares, they need to be taught to recognize this and take authority over the evil thoughts or nightmares and tell them to stop. They are to cast them out in the name of Jesus Christ who has all authority over the evil kingdom. If we tolerate bad thoughts coming in and meditate on them, we are basically allowing them to stay. Our mind is ours to protect and the mind of a child needs to be protected by the child and the parents are a big part of this protection. If dreams, thoughts, and imaginations are in conflict with what God's word says, they must go. God does not tell us to tolerate evil but to expose it and remove it from ourselves and our households.

H.) <u>Love God, love others, love yourself</u>; *"Jesus said unto him, 'Thou shalt love the Lord thy God with all thy heart, and with all thy soul, and with all thy mind. This is the first and great commandment. And the second is like unto it, Thou shalt love thy neighbor as thyself."* (Matthew 22:37-39)

I.) <u>Guard your heart</u>; *"Keep thy heart with all diligence; for out of it are the issues of life."* (Proverbs 4:23)

The children's hearts need to be guarded. It is unhelpful to a child to bury their emotional pain. As parents or guardians of the child, we can help them work through the pain in their hearts. If a child never works through or casts off their emotional pain, it can cause soul wounds and later affect them again and again because of the pain already buried. This can make them unable to handle new difficult situations in life that arise because of the pain that already exists buried in their heart.

Children need to be taught God's word and that God's word commands us to forgive others and ourselves and to not hold bitterness (ought) towards others. These are commands in the word of God and if children respond out of their own wounded heart and not what God says, this can be a big stumbling block for them. If they start building up unforgiveness, bitterness, or resentment towards others, God, or themselves at a young age, the lies keep piling up and sin will get a foothold. Our hearts need a spiritual heart surgery where God pulls out the lies, and we receive the truth.

J.) The Holy Spirit

God has given the child a conscience to protect them. Children have the word of God and the Holy Spirit to guide them in life. Teaching a child to read the Bible and obey the leading of the Holy Spirit is extremely important for their spiritual walk. How does a child know if they are hearing the Holy Spirit? The Holy Spirit will never speak to a child anything that goes against the word of God. According to 1 Kings 19:12, God's voice sounds like a still small voice. God does not hurry us, does not rush us, and does not pressure us. Furthermore, His voice is peaceful and truthful (word of God). His words will empower us to obey Him, reveal His love to us, and give us a sound mind. As a child learns to cast off bad thoughts and evil imaginations, the child will be able to hear the voice of the Holy Spirit better. Children need to be taught that if they are having bad thoughts, they need to tell the thought to stop. If bad thoughts are coming in, they are not from God and should not be put up with but cast off and not tolerated. The child is in control of their mind and what is allowed in their imagination. If they have dark thoughts and don't want them, they are responsible to cast them out. Don't allow the enemy to get a foothold by ruminating on evil imaginations. This is where order in the home is vitally important, and the parents need to pray over their children's mind. That is why having deep meaningful conversations with our children is important because we can discern whether unhealthy thoughts are going on in their heads. Another important aspect in hearing the Holy Spirit is the quietness of their environment. If a child is always in a loud and chaotic environment, it is harder to hear the Holy Spirit. Therefore, giving our children a peaceful home life and knowing what type of environment they have at school or with friends is important.

Finally, the word of God says in 1 Corinthians 2:13-14, *"Which things also we speak, not in the words which man's wisdom teaches, but which the Holy Spirit teaches; comparing spiritual things with spiritual. But the natural man receives not the things of the Spirit of God: for they are foolishness unto him: neither can he know then, because they are spiritually discerned."* Amen.

K.) Waking up to the Spiritual Holy War

We are spiritual beings which means we have a spirit, and we will live forever either in heaven or hell. There are two spiritual kingdoms warring for each person's soul. Jesus died on the cross for you and for your children to be freed from the bondage of sin and death. Satan is looking around the earth for who he can devour. If we are ignorant of this, how can we fight spiritually for our children if we don't truly believe there is an evil kingdom working 24/7.

Satan is the father of lies and one of his lies is to convince children that they are without choices. Even though children are under the authority of their parents, to guide and protect them, children still have many choices to make. They choose to obey or not to obey their parents and God. They choose to willingly do their schoolwork with their best effort or not. They choose to spend their time wisely or not. It is important not to be ignorant of Satan's lies and deceptions and to recognize the importance of your choices whether adult or child. If you are feeling caged in, boxed in, or made to feel you have no choices, that is from Satan. Whether it is a child or an adult experiencing this, it is time for spiritual warfare. Here are a few scriptures you can proclaim and confess aloud; *"For God has not given us the spirit of fear; but of power, and of love, and of a sound mind."* (2 Timothy 1:7) Also Ephesians 6:13 and Ephesians 6:16. *"Wherefore take to you the whole armor of God, that you may be able to withstand in the evil day, and having done all, to stand." "Above all, taking the shield of faith, wherewith you shall be able to quench (put out, extinguish) all the fiery darts (arrows, shots) of the wicked."*

L. The Power of the Imagination

How do we teach our children to use their imagination for good? Let's look at Philippians 4:8, *"Finally, brethren, whatsoever things are true, whatsoever things are honest, whatsoever things are just, whatsoever things are pure, whatsoever things are lovely, whatsoever things are of good report; if there be any virtue, and if there be any praise, think on these things."* Therefore, we are to use our imagination to think of things that are true, honest, just, pure, lovely, of good report, virtuous, and praiseworthy. Furthermore, when we have a clear conscience, we will know what is true and virtuous. If someone's conscience has been seared, they will most likely be using their imagination for things that are not true and not virtuous. Therefore, how does someone who has a seared conscience return their conscience to a pure and clear conscience? The word of God is quick and powerful and is a discerner of the thoughts and intents of the heart. The LORD heals and restores what is broken in His children as we cry out to Him with a sincere heart (repentance). How do we draw a lost child into the mysteries of God and out of the deceptions of the world? I believe one important point to remember is that Jesus said to bring the children to Him. We should not hide things in scripture that we think are too hard for a child to understand. When a child knows the truth, the truth will set them free. If they never hear the uncompromised truth in the word of God, how can they break free of the lying chains of the world. For example, if a child is interested in reading books about vampires, now is the time to teach them about the good and evil kingdoms. When we don't share the uncompromised truth in scripture, we are only giving children partial truth. We are in a war, a holy war! As children learn to listen to the Holy Spirit, the Holy Spirit will teach them what the word of God means. Children are exposed to things from other children, television, video games, books, social media, etc., and if they don't have deep spiritual truths to guide them, they won't know how to handle life's issues correctly. The world will teach our children things that they don't know how to process by themselves. They need daily parental involvement in what is going on in their thoughts and hearts. If children receive evil thoughts in their head and just think they have to put up with it, this is detrimental to them. Teaching children, as well as a person of any age, to cast off anxiety, fear, and evil imaginations is vital to the believer's walk of faith.

We will now look at an example of a game that is a spiritual trap. Let's look at an article from Focus on the Family, "<u>Parental Concerns About 'Dungeons and Dragons</u>'". This article states there are strong occult components to the game. Past players of the game indicated that their involvement in the game brought demonic activity into their life. Parents indicate their serious concern about the 48-hour marathon games that are played. During these marathons, players sometimes don't eat or sleep. Some of the players of Dungeons and Dragons become addicted to the game and are addicted to residing as a character in a fantasy world. This game is not the only game that is a spiritual trap. There are video games and other fantasy board games that draw our youth into wasting away their minutes, hours, years, and in some cases decades of their life by these games that open doors to the dark spiritual world. The dark forces behind these activities lead children into addictions, hopelessness, laziness, depression, anti-social behavior, and lack of motivation. These games are not harmless games but evil tricks of manipulation and control over our youth to waste away their time, life, imagination, and creativity.

M.) <u>Do not keep darkness hidden</u>!

Children need to know that they can come to their parents or other trusted adults to discuss anything. If our children are having dark thoughts, nightmares, or whatever else they may be struggling with, they need to know they can come to their parents, guardians, or other loved ones and talk about spiritual struggles and not only share their victories but work through their defeats. Children need to know the power of bringing the darkness into the light and not hiding their struggles. By bringing the darkness to the kitchen table of discussion and not allowing the lies to continue, is life-changing and the bond you build with your child is priceless. Children need to know that it is not a failure on their part that evil is bombarding them, but it is something to be acknowledged in order to be defeated.

CHAPTER 15:
WORDS MATTER

The words our children meditate on and imagine have an impact on their lives. I am sure you have heard the saying, "Sticks and stones may break your bones, but words will never hurt you." This old rhyme was used to defend against name-calling, but the truth is that words have power whether good or bad. The word of God says that life and death are in the power of the tongue. The power of our tongue is in the words we speak. The words we speak to others and ourselves have power. Children need to be taught the truth about the words they speak.

There is a song "O Be Careful, Little Eyes" by Cedarmont Kids. This is a song full of lyrics that teach a great lesson to children. Some of the truth-speaking lyrics are: "O be careful little ears what you hear." "O be careful little tongue what you say." "O be careful little hands what you do." "O be careful little feet where you go." "O be careful little heart whom you trust." "O be careful little mind what you think." These lyrics are a good way for a child to meditate on powerful truth. Children learn things very easily through song. This song will help teach them to be mindful of what they are listening to, what they are speaking, what they are participating in, and what is going on in their heart.

There is a common saying, "Time heals all wounds." This is not true and if children are led to believe it is, it can stop them from sharing their feelings. They may bury wounds and hurts thinking they will just go away after time. Our Heavenly Father wants our souls healed and healthy, and the word of God tells us how to keep our souls healthy. When children understand that the word of God commands us to forgive others so our sins can be forgiven, children can be set free from the bondage that occurs when we don't forgive others. The word of God also says that envy rots the bones. When children are taught the scripture, they are able to protect their souls, mind, and body by following the word of God.

CHAPTER 16:
THE POWER OF A STORY

The little ones love to hear interesting stories. The adults in their lives can choose what kind of stories they read to them. There are many children's stories that are scary for children, and I am not sure why they have lasted over the years. I had this interesting story I was reading in the classroom. I was quite pleased by the overall interest from the whole class as I read this book. It was about a boy who was really upset with his family, and he gave his family the silent treatment. He was saying that he hated his family. The story was very direct in explaining his emotions and his anger. The boy worked through his emotions throughout the book and finally, the boy decided to forgive his family. Many of the children in my classroom wanted to share their own stories of being upset with their family and how they worked through their feelings about it. Overall, it was a wonderfully healing day for the students as many of them were intrigued by the story and could relate to the boy's feelings in the story and how he worked through his emotions. There was one boy in my classroom who was working through his own family dynamics, and he was having a lot of difficulty processing the breakup of his family. This young boy listened intently to the details of the story and was the first to want to share his feelings about how he forgave his family when he was angry with them. He talked about how his dad made him feel better and helped him work through his emotions.

The valuable lesson in this children's book was about being honest about your feelings. This little boy in the book was very blunt and honest about how his family hurt him. Being truthful is part of the healing process and this book helped teach children the importance of that and the importance of forgiveness. When the child buries their feelings deep in their soul, this is very unhealthy and usually leads to the child having layers of soul wounds over time.

In my classroom, I would share stories of fond memories of my youth with my classroom, and they truly enjoyed hearing them. I would share with my students how when I was younger, I would lace up my ice skates and walk down the hill next to our house. At the bottom of the hill, a beautifully flat ice-skating rink would naturally form in the winter. When there was a calm winter evening, I would happily skate for hours under the moonlit sky. My memory of the beauty of these still winter evenings with the glistening moon on the ice rink still makes me smile inside. Part of this beautiful memory was because of my mom since she always helped me tighten my skates, so they fit perfectly. Sharing stories with our children of childhood memories is a great bonding experience with them. Helping children use their imaginations to imagine the story in their minds is a powerful tool. Our imagination can be used to help us through tough moments in life where if we imagine something lovely, it helps us get through tough moments.

CHAPTER 17:
WHO IS INFLUENCING YOUR CHILD?

Who is your child learning from and asking their questions to? *"My son, keep my father's commandment, and forsake not the law of thy mother"* (Proverbs 6:20). I had a first-grade student who while standing in line to go to lunch said to me, "Can a man marry a man?" Who is supposed to answer this question? Would you want your child's teacher answering these types of questions or would you want to answer them? Is the church helping parents navigate these questions? Doesn't the Bible answer these questions? Let's look at what the Bible says about this. The scripture says that the imagination of the thoughts of the heart was evil continually. Scripture also says to cast down evil imaginations. When we look at Sodom and Gomorrah, there were men lusting after men. These men's imaginations were evil and led them to acts of evil. If our children are confused, there are many biblical stories we can use to teach them what is right and wrong. With all the evil imaginations trying to indoctrinate our children, we need to have the tools of scripture in our hands to battle the evil imaginations that try to invade our children's minds. Leviticus 20:13 says, *"If a man also lie with mankind, as he lies with a woman, both of them have committed an abomination…"* Also, Romans 1:26-27, *"For this cause God gave them up to vile affections: for even their women did change the natural use into that which is against nature. And likewise also the men, leaving the natural use of the woman, burned in their lust one toward another; men with men working that which is unseemly, and receiving in themselves that recompense (penalty) of their error which was meet (fitting)."*

Music lyrics and even music rhythms can influence a child's imagination. If you hear lyrics such as "the memories of the past haunt me and I won't forget them", or "I will not let go of what you have done to me", or "I will get revenge; you will pay for what you have done."; these words have an effect on you. Hearing lyrics like these over and over again can cause us to imagine and meditate on bad emotions and lead to depression, bitterness, or unforgiveness in our hearts. Meditating on past unhealthy emotions can lead our minds down a dangerous trail. We can start to feel extremely sad when hearing a song with sad lyrics. Music can influence our emotions; and, therefore, lead our emotions into anger or depression just by listening to a song that brings our imagination into remembering a past negative memory which can be troublesome to our soul.

It is important that we evaluate the music we are listening to because it can affect our mood; it can affect our choices. Years ago, I saw a music tour bus in Chicago that had a large cobra, in attack mode, on the side of the bus. Cobras can stand for dark spiritual things in different cultures. This tour bus belonged to a very famous music artist. The work this music artist did at that time was fine to many people. I questioned this music artist's intentions because of the music lyrics that were consistent in the songs. A lot of these music lyrics were about bitterness and revenge. Do we want our children to listen to music that brings their imagination into a place of bitterness or revenge, anger, unforgiveness, passionate desires, or depression? As time has passed, probably ten years, this same music artist now has dark spiritual stage performances; what some Christians say are Satanic rituals. We cannot be ignorant of Satan's devices and what we are exposing our youth to.

There are many ways things in our world can influence our children. But the main point to remember is that your influence as an active, faith-filled, praying parent is more powerful than the world's influence. Your truthfulness and open discussions with your children about questions they have will have a much greater impact than ignoring or avoiding them. The Holy Spirit will guide faithful parents on what to say during difficult discussions. This world exposes our children to many things but bringing the darkness into the light breaks the power of the darkness.

CHAPTER 18:
BRINGING PEACE TO THE CHILDREN

There is a lot to learn and observe from the middle school classrooms. Many middle school classrooms have various transitions during the day. This particular classroom had seven different transitions and three of these classes were loud and rowdy. Large classroom sizes and boisterous classrooms are not uncommon. If you are a quieter child, these middle school and high school classrooms can be overwhelming.

Too much noise can become overwhelming and can result in anger, frustration, recluse behavior, etc. This day in middle school was excessively loud and there was no peace in the classroom. I would guess that about 60-70% of the students were unable to complete their assignments due to a lack of motivation and classroom noise. I had tried all my usual methods to get the students' attention, and the room would be quiet for a short time and then would go back to the excessive noise. This was partially due to the large classroom size. There are some students who seem to thrive in loud classrooms, but, in general, it causes inefficient use of time and disorder. Out of my spirit,

Denise White

I said to this middle school classroom *"Peace, peace be still!"* I heard a student say, *"Jesus said that to calm the storm."* When I speak to the chaos, peace will come when I am persistent. One important lesson I have learned through my years of teaching is that I need to believe in myself as a teacher, and I need to believe in the spiritual authority I have to speak to the mountains in my life and the classroom. I need to bring peace and light wherever I go.

This next day of school events included a storm and bringing peace during a storm. It was a cold windy day with 40 mph winds. Zoe, a fourth grader, was talking about how scared she is of storms. She was talking in detail about thunderstorms, tornadoes, winter storms, etc. She and a few other students kept going over to the windows and gasping as the wind gusts were extremely strong. Then Zoe began talking about how she is not only afraid of storms but that she is going to die young. I told the students to stop going to the window and that it is windy out but there was no thunderstorm or tornado. I could see how the students were building up their fear as they talked about their fears. Many other things were going on in the classroom and four paraprofessionals were all assisting since this was a large class. I waited for my opportunity to talk to Zoe. My opportunity came and I told her to speak to the fear and say "stop". She said she can't stop the thoughts. The truth is we do have authority over our thoughts and the devil will put thoughts in our mind. The children need to know that they are to resist and fight against bad thoughts. We are to speak to our mountain. In this case, the mountain is evil thoughts. Therefore, speak to the evil thoughts. Zoe could say, "No, I will not die young. I will live a full long life." The word of God says we do not have a spirit of fear, but of power, love, and sound mind. Therefore, fear is a spirit. We need to choose to say no to that spirit and not let it have access. We need to be careful of what we agree with (what agreements have we made in writing, in our words, in our heart, or our thoughts/imagination). The battle in the mind is real and requires speaking scripture aloud, choosing to fight against the devil's lies, and closing any open doors to the devil's lies. For example, if Zoe is allowed to watch horror movies or if her family allows other fear-inducing things into the home, they need to stop allowing her to be influenced by this darkness and simply not allow her to watch horror movies. It is also important to know what other influences the child has in their life. This classroom had skeleton characters from a well-known nightmare movie on every wall. Even the clock on the wall was from this nightmare movie. We were given common sense to use it and things encouraging "nightmares" can bring them. It is important to assess the environment we are in and how that environment affects us. Children are very susceptible to these things because the devil starts to train people when they are young. I encourage parents to be vigilant in knowing the environments their children are in and to pay attention to any changes in their children and what environment has been influencing them.

Denise White

What are some other ways we can bring peace to our children? We can be vigilant in using our common sense when buying merchandise for our home and the clothing we wear. We have many choices for merchandise in America. It does take discernment and time to sort through the choices. For instance, when we go to buy clothing for our children, what words or pictures are on their clothing? Two boys had the same shirt on in their kindergarten class. The shirts said "venom" and were dark with scary pictures of snakes and unusual creatures. Additionally, and much more extreme, was in a middle school classroom where the teacher had transformed her classroom into Hogwarts. You walk into her classroom and there is a Hogwarts flag, there was a long cane with a snake head, a witch's broom, skulls on sticks, snakes on sticks, wands, figurines saying "dementor", figurines of dragons, necklaces with swords and evil symbols, and the walls resembled Hogwarts. For some people, these things may seem fun, harmless, and entertaining. But if you truly use your God-given discernment and assess it, you will recognize these objects and entertainment are anything but harmless.

Engaging in witchcraft and magic is clearly stated in the Bible as divination and is not to be part of the believer's life. The world tries to portray these objects as entertaining and fun for the imagination, but the truth is *"the imagination of man's heart is evil from his youth"* (Genesis 8:21). Let's look at some further verses about the imagination of men: *"And God saw that the wickedness of man was great in the earth, and that every imagination of the thoughts of his heart was only evil continually."* (Genesis 6:5) *"But they hearkened not, nor inclined their ear; but walked in the counsels and in the imagination of their evil heart, and went backward, and not forward."* (Jeremiah 7:24) *"Casting down imaginations, and every high (proud) thing that exalts itself against the knowledge of God and bringing into captivity every thought to the obedience of Christ."* (2 Corinthians 10:5)

Are we bringing light or darkness into our homes? Are we bringing peace or trouble to our home with what we allow into our home? Let's look at evaluating the presence of witchcraft, magic, and sorcery in television, movies, books, clothing, and other objects. If you have ever seen a magic show, they are really trying to trick your mind. We are told by God to guard our mind and when we allow magicians or sorcerers to trick us and deceive us, this can lead us down the wrong path of being deceived and can affect our clarity of mind. Whether it be black magic or white magic, it is still magic meant to deceive. Black magic involves the summoning of evil spirits for evil purposes. White magic seems to be defined differently in various places but generally, it is "if it does no harm, do your own will". This is basically saying if you aren't hurting anyone, do what you feel like doing. Some people who engage in white magic worship nature and are wiccans. No matter what you call it, magic is divination, and God strongly speaks of the dangers in scripture. It is not harmless but an opening into the dark evils of Satan. One dangerous game that I have heard children speak of recently was the Ouija board game. These games are opening the door to evil. If you have played this game and have now realized it was wrong, simply go to the LORD and repent (change of mind). When we come to the knowledge of the truth in an area, we will sorrowfully repent to our LORD. Ask the LORD to help remove you from dangerous things you may have participated in or been exposed to. Ask the LORD to restore your peace. Witchcraft, magic, sorcery, etc. play tricks on the mind and bring confusion and disorder to your thoughts. What does the Bible say about these things? Galatians 5:19-21 says, *"Now the works of the flesh are manifest, which are these; adultery, fornication, uncleanness, lasciviousness (sensuality), idolatry, witchcraft, hatred, variance (discord), emulations (jealousy), wrath, strife, seditions (dissensions), heresies, envying, murders, drunkenness, revellings, and such like: of the which I tell you before, as I have also told you in time past, that they which do such things shall not inherit the kingdom of God."*

The LORD's peace which is found in Him, and the word of God is not of this world. When we teach our children the truths of scripture, we will bring peace and order into their minds. Satan's objects of occult and divination bring chaos and confusion to the mind. God brings peace and order by His word and by the Holy Spirit.

Keeping the peace for our children will involve helping them work through the daily challenges and events that occur. After children come home from school or a friend's house, it is a good idea to sit down and have a chat. Ask them to tell you about their day, and as they share their experiences and feelings, you will know how to help them process and work through their day. Then this would be a great time to teach them how to pray over their mind and heart.

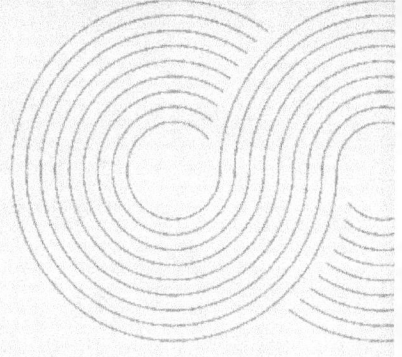

CHAPTER 19:

NURTURING THE CHILD'S IMAGINATION

What are some activities that will nurture a pure and healthy imagination for a child:

- According to Psalm 150, let everything that has breath praise the LORD. This can include singing, dancing, or musical instruments.

- Teach your child how to plant a garden. You can include your favorite vegetables and herbs or plant a flower garden. This can also teach a child the biblical principles about sowing and reaping, and about producing good fruit and harvesting.

- According to Mark 10:14, "...*Allow the little children to come to Me and forbid them not: for of such is the kingdom of God.*" Therefore, any activity that brings the child to the LORD to learn His kingdom's truths is beneficial. Such as family Bible studies, family prayer time, Vacation Bible School, Sunday School, home Bible studies, baptism, church, praying, etc.

Denise White

- Family time to play while encouraging meaningful conversation.

- Creative time to build, design, etc.

- Teach your children life skills such as cooking, laundry, cleaning, and using this activity as a way to build relationships.

- Making and eating dinner together while having conversation about the joys and disappointments of the day while helping them work through any thoughts, emotions, or experiences of the day.

- Discuss with your child their talents and giftings. Tell your child what makes them special. Have them make a list of activities they may want to pursue.

- Teach them biblical principles. For example, forgiveness, mercy for mercy, what it means to trust in the LORD, and knowing their identity in Christ.

- Teach them to have a generous heart by giving to someone in need or doing a task together that blesses someone.

- Spend time just listening to them.

- Have a map hanging on the wall of the United States or a world map and mark places you want to visit and places you have already visited.

- Have an arts and craft area where you collect items that can be used to make projects.
- Teach them to cook and other life skills. Examples could be meal planning, cooking together, kitchen clean-up and organization, grocery shopping, budgeting, and saving, etc.
- If your child likes to design or be an architect, you can work together to build a diorama of a home or farm.
- You and your child can create or repair something. You could watch a YouTube video to show you how to make something new or repair something broken.
- Teach your child a skill you learned when you were young.
- Have game night and maybe include games like Life or Monopoly.
- Plan and prepare a picnic for the whole family.
- Plan and create a scavenger hunt as a family and invite family and friends to join in on the fun.
- Have your children write a letter to a family member who lives far away.
- On your child's birthday or near their birthday each year, make plans to help them nurture and practice their talents and giftings.

- Do a physical activity together with your child. It could be a sporting activity, a hike, a camping trip, playing at a park, bicycling, etc.

- Make a list as a family of everything you are grateful for.

- Get your children a journal to record their experiences, ideas, and as a tool to help them work through their emotions. If they are too young to write, they can draw pictures.

- Help your children discern good entertainment from unhealthy entertainment and why it is important to discern the difference.

- Help your child to recognize the Holy Spirit, their thoughts, and the thoughts Satan is trying to put in their mind. Teach them to cast off evil imaginations. Romans 8:14-16, *"For as many as are led by the Spirit of God, they are the sons of God. For you have not received the spirit of bondage again to fear; but you have received the Spirit of adoption, whereby we cry, Abba, Father. The Spirit Itself bears witness with our spirit, that we are the children of God."*

- Teach your children about the importance of having a relationship with God and how to stay close to God.

- Discuss the qualities of a good friend.

- Plan family adventures together.

- Teach your children how to worship God.

- Learn about God's beautiful creation of animals and nature. Examples could be visiting a farm, zoo, or going to the lake.
- Play athletic games with minimal competition to instill the importance of enjoying a game versus being the best.
- Teach your children how to pray.
- Watch inspirational, Christian, or similar shows together and discuss the morals displayed in the show.
- Teach your children how to take care of pets, or volunteer at the Humane Society.
- Have a talent show with singing, dancing, comedy, gymnastics, playing an instrument, sport skills, etc.
- Have a book club and discuss the morals of the book and also discuss what they would change in the story if they could rewrite it.
- Tell stories as a family either making up stories or recalling great family memories.
- Have game night and add one new rule to the game or create a whole new game.
- Take a household problem, discuss possible solutions, and decide as a family which solution will work best to solve the problem.
- Choose a scripture verse and discuss the biblical principle it teaches.

- Enjoy the outdoors by going on an outdoor adventure looking for birds or forest creatures.

- Use your imagination and find a way to bless someone in need.

- Together discuss Habakkuk 2:2 and write a plan (vision) for each child's future. Habakkuk 2:2, *"Then the LORD answered me and said, 'write the vision and make it plain on tablets. That he may run who reads it.'"*

- Create ways to bring the Bible alive to your children. Examples: act out a story from the Bible; read the parable of the prodigal son and discuss the meaning; work together to create the full armor of God from craft items you have at home; ask family members to share their favorite verse from the Bible; play a game of charades acting out different stories, parables, disciples, or words from the Bible; play a game of Pictionary drawing pictures of miracles in the Bible, etc.

- As a family, join together to discuss issues that involve the entire family and problem solve as a family. Begin this time together in prayer. Teaching your children to have healthy communication is a great life skill.

Have fun coming up with creative ways to nurture your child and family's imagination. You can have a list on the refrigerator that your children can add their ideas to. Enjoy your family as you stretch their imagination!

CHAPTER 20:

NOT HINDERING THE CHILDREN FROM THE KINGDOM

We inherit the kingdom of God like a little child. When we are children, we get quite excited about little and big things. Something I have noticed about elementary students versus middle school and high school students, when an elementary student leaves early for the day all the other classmates want to hug the student leaving. Whereas the students in middle or high school are not really as interested or excited as the younger children. The enthusiasm of a young child is extraordinary; something as simple as finding a rock outside that is unique can make a young child smile from ear to ear. It was a lovely sight when I was in the store parking lot and this three-year-old boy was walking with his grandfather. They were both quite sweet and the little boy found something on the ground that drew his curiosity, and the grandfather said, "Oh wow!" Children have a wonderful ability to display joy and enthusiasm for life.

Forbid them not: Luke 18:16-17, *"But Jesus called them to Him and said, Let the little children come to Me, and do not forbid them: for of such is the kingdom of God. Assuredly, I say to you, whosoever does not receive the kingdom of God as a little child will by no means enter it."* Jesus wants us to bring the little children to Him. He wants us to teach our children about Him. There are many children that recite songs from movies and sing along happily but something amazingly special is when a child knows the word of God and recites scripture. I was watching a minister of the gospel of Jesus Christ on YouTube, and he was with a family that received deliverance. The two young brothers were reciting Psalm 35. The older boy who was maybe 7 years old would recite one verse and then the younger brother who was maybe 5 would recite it after him. They recited all 28 verses. It brought me so much joy to hear this. It was a priceless gift to see these brothers ministering to all the people at the conference and to everyone that would see this YouTube video. In the United States, it is common to hear children join together and sing a popular movie song, but can you imagine the power if we were to hear a group of children break out reciting scripture.

I had the pleasure of knowing these three six-year-old students named: Ian, Lee, and Daniel. They were all first graders with faith in Jesus Christ who attended an elementary school that did not practice faith in school. Lee brought his Bible to school often. Ian was quite intelligent but tended to tell white lies. Daniel was a unique boy who struggled with being critical of himself. All three of these boys had faith in Jesus Christ, and all three of these boys struggled with the thoughts in their minds. Lee was always complaining about other students and what they said or did to him. Ian told a lot of lies about activities he did to impress the student or teacher. Daniel really struggled with disappointment and the expectations at school. Each of these boys at one time or another shared with me their faith in God. I loved hearing their testimonies in class. When they shared their struggles with me, I took that as an open door to share the truth of Jesus Christ. I tried to help these three boys with recognizing their thoughts and casting down imaginations. I had opportunity to pray for Lee, and he had earlier shared that his favorite verse was *"Trust in the LORD with all your heart"*, and I used this verse to pray for him. Daniel was watching and listening to me pray for Lee, and he said, "Yes, that is right, trust in the LORD!" These boys were precious and gave me such joy to see and hear of their faith. All three of these boys had struggles with their thoughts and did not know how to cast off their dark thoughts. In my experience in Sunday School and children's church, I have not heard children taught about casting off imaginations. These three children were special in their giftings and needed encouragement in that. Unfortunately, in a classroom with 30 plus students, I was unable to nurture each student's gifts the way I would want to. Lee, Ian, and Daniel were all intelligent, creative thinkers, and had spiritual awareness without knowing how to handle their spiritual sensitivity.

Jesus said to let the children come to Him and do not forbid them. Teaching our children the principles of the Kingdom of God is essential for them to know how to navigate this earthly world full of temptations. The lies of this world and the fiery darts (arrows) of Satan's kingdom does affect the children, especially the children who do not know the principles of scripture. Ephesians 6 says to put on the whole armor of God in order that we can stand against the trickery of the devil. Our children need to be prepared with their full armor because the wicked day will come, and they need to be ready to stand. Church attendance alone does not mean the child is prepared and ready for battle against Satan. The child needs to have a relationship with Jesus and talk (pray) to Him. The parents are to train their child up to know the LORD personally by studying the scripture and being taught Biblical principles of the Bible. The child's imagination needs to be guarded by parents, and the child needs to be taught how to protect their mind, thoughts, and imagination.

I believe there is a real need to teach children the deep truths of scripture. Do children learn how to cast down lying thoughts? Do children learn how to cast off evil imaginations that come into their minds? Are children hearing more about fantasy and fairytale movies than from God's word? Do children know the Biblical principles of the Bible? Do children know the truths about Jesus Christ well enough to share them with someone else? The Bible is truth, and the world is full of lies and deception in movies, songs, video games, etc. that children are exposed to. When the Bible is taught in its entirety, our children have spiritual ammunition to fight the lies of Satan coming at them in different directions.

There is incredible power when a child knows the word of God and can share it. I had two boys in a small class. Jake was spending weeks writing a story about the life of Jesus. He wrote about the birth of Jesus, the first miracle of Jesus, healing stories where Jesus healed the sick and raised the dead, and the crucifixion and resurrection of Jesus Christ. One day he read his story to Nathan who was a 3rd grader and Jake was a first grader. After Jake read his beautiful story of the life of Jesus to Nathan, Nathan said to Jake, "I go to church every Sunday, and I didn't know any of that." Jake was homeschooled, and his mom and dad taught him all about the life of Jesus. We are responsible for teaching our children about Jesus. The church is the backup, not the frontlines.

CHAPTER 21:
RESTORING ORDER TO THE CHILD'S MIND AND SOUL

Some classrooms are oversized, and the level of noise is so high that the teacher must strain her voice to speak loud enough for the students to hear. I am sure there could be many reasons for the loud noise level, but in general, it could very well be from the stressors in children's lives, the stressors in the teacher's life, and the stressors at the school overall. I taught in a classroom where there were 41 students. You can imagine how challenging that classroom was to maintain order. I wonder if a student feels "heard" in a classroom of 30-plus students. From my experience, when a child feels valued and heard in the classroom and life, they are much more likely to be a healthy and happy child.

Helping to restore order to a child's life and boldly teaching them the truth is essential. I truly enjoyed the relationship I built with this seven-year-old. He had a really great sense of humor and always made me smile and laugh. He was writing a story about Takis which is a spicy chip. A line in his story read, "My friend sprinkled Takis dust on my lunch and ever since then,

Denise White

I love Takis." That is kind of like what Satan does he sprinkles a little lie here and a little lie there hoping we buy into what he is selling. The enemy sprinkles a lie into our minds to ease us into his deceptions. Don't receive the sprinkling of his lies; resist Satan and he will flee.

How do we restore order to the child's mind and soul? How do we help our children become whole in their minds and souls? I have often seen children with learning delays who have some emotional, social, or family issues that need addressing. Sometimes when we slow down and listen to these children, we may be able to help them work through some of what is troubling their hearts. Anxiety, worry, and unprocessed emotional concerns may take up needed brain space. Therefore, when the child can work through his thoughts and concerns, he is then better able to focus on learning better with less brain energy spent on worry. Dismissing or ignoring a child's emotions does not help them, but addressing their concerns and creating a safe place for them to share their heart is a helpful starting point. Even if we have no idea what to do to help our children with pain or hurt in their souls, we can listen to them and let them know we love them unconditionally like our Father in heaven loves us. We can teach our children to talk to God about anything.

I want to share with you a beautiful story of a young boy being set free and how order was restored to him and his family. This testimony is from Above & Beyond Christian Counseling and is titled "Praying Deliverance for Small Children" by Phyllis Tarbox. A husband and wife brought in their 4-year-old son to a Christian counseling center that does deliverance. Their son had severe defiance problems, and they were concerned about possible violence towards their younger son. The counselor talked to the parents separately and witnessed for herself the unusual behavior of the boy. Before this meeting with the counselor, the parents knew of deliverance and prayed to break generational curses off of their son but still had not been able to help their son. The 4-year-old said, "I do not want you to pray for me." This was odd because they had not even suggested that yet. The parents shared that their son has told them not to do that binding and loosing prayer and that he didn't want them to put scripture on his bedroom wall which the parents tried to do but the boy insisted they come down. After gathering all this information, the counselor was praying a deliverance prayer and when they got to the place where they were calling out a spirit of murder and violence, the boy started choking. After gently calling this out over and over in Jesus' name, he coughed, and it came out. Apparently, when the boy was in daycare, another child tried to choke him, and the evil spirit entered the boy at that time through his throat. Then when the boy was delivered from the evil spirit, the evil spirit left the way it came in, through the throat. Through the deliverance prayer, the ungodly soul tie with that daycare child was broken. Furthermore, when the boy was defiant about anyone praying for him and when he insisted that no scriptures be put on his bedroom wall, this was the evil spirit speaking through the boy because the boy couldn't even read yet. This Christian counseling center helped this family tremendously as they applied what the scripture says. This Christian counseling center believed in setting the captive free and new the truth. When we know the truth from the word of God, we apply the word of God by faith to our situations. We are to speak to our mountains. Children need to be set free as well as adults. Freedom and deliverance are the children's bread according to scripture. It is our portion which is freedom. Jesus died on the cross not only for our salvation but for our freedom from oppression here on earth.

How does the LORD speak to His children? One way He speaks to us is through dreams. We can receive dreams and visions from God. According to Joel 2:28, *"And it shall come to pass afterward that I will pour out My Spirit upon all flesh, and your sons and your daughters shall prophesy, your old men shall dream dreams, your young men shall see visions."* Children can receive warning dreams. According to Matthew 2:12, the wise men were warned in a dream not to return to Herod. Herod wanted the wise men to lead him to find baby Jesus and wanted to kill Jesus. In verse 13 of Matthew 2, the angel of the Lord appeared to Joseph in a dream telling him to flee into Egypt with Mary and baby Jesus. It is important for us to talk with our children about their dreams. If our children tell us they have a dream or nightmare, we should ask them about it and write the dream down. We should pray with our child and ask the LORD the meaning of the dream. The child or the parent may have discernment as to what the dream means. If there is something going on in the child's life, God may be trying to give them direction or a warning. Dreams are one way God speaks to us and speaks to the children.

CHAPTER 22:
BE AN INFLUENCER

We should be influencing people to follow the truth not the imaginations of the world. People will watch how we handle situations in our life. When we glorify God in the good times and in the difficult times, we are testifying of His goodness. You never know who is watching you; your actions can influence people. Social media can be a very fake reality and the influencers on social media will mostly show you the favorable side of their life. We don't usually get to witness how they are in their everyday life and how they react to difficult circumstances. Children learn a lot from other children, especially from their actions. Children can learn good and bad behaviors from other children. That is why it is so important to know the friends our children are spending time with.

When our children are raised to follow Jesus Christ, they will be influencers to other children. I had a student who was sharing a story with the class about what he did over Easter weekend. This student said to the class, "Did you know that God raised His Son from the dead!" This student said this statement with such amazement; it was truly beautiful to hear! Another student of mine, Layton, was struggling one day with his emotions. Layton was a believer in Jesus Christ and had shared with me earlier that his favorite verse was *"Trust in the LORD with all your heart"*. I asked Layton if I could pray for him, and he said yes. I used Layton's favorite verse in the prayer and another boy named David heard the prayer and said, "Yep, what Mrs. White said is true." These boys were precious as David helped encourage Layton in his time of need. These types of stories you may not always hear, but when children know the LORD, they walk around blessing others beautifully as they influence those around them.

We can influence other parents by training our children in the LORD and parenting according to God's standard not the world's standard. Not only can the parents be influencers, but the child's influence can make a huge impact. The voice of one little child can speak louder than a group of adults. When a believing child learns to speak truth in love, that child's voice will echo and impact many, as life is in the power of the tongue. When a child recites scripture out of their spirit, it softens the room and sends an important message of the power of the faith of a believing child. *"But He said, leave the children alone! Allow the little ones to come to Me, and do not forbid or restrain or hinder them, for of such as these is the Kingdom of Heaven composed."* (Matthew 19:14 Amplified classic)

CONCLUSION-ACTION PLAN

The family is precious to the LORD and the devil walks about seeking to devour the family. We are to be vigilant, watching carefully for the traps the devil is setting for our children. As parents, we have a responsibility to guard and protect our children, but children also have a responsibility to cast off evil imaginations and honor their parents. Each person in the family has a responsibility and decides what kingdom they will serve. That is why discipline is vitally important for our children, to save their soul from the pit.

Guarding your child's imagination requires strategies and to be proactive. Being uninformed about your child's activities, friends, or their thought life is unwise. Likewise having no game plan to guard your child's imagination is counterproductive. Therefore, let's get started right away with a plan.

List below the steps you will take to teach your children biblical principles including teaching them to cast off evil imaginations. (2 Corinthians 10:4-6)

_____

_____

With the information you have gained from this book, list below things that are in your child's life that are detrimental to their imagination.

_____

_____

_____

_____

_____

_____

List below the steps you will take to guard your child's imagination. For example, what activities need to be removed from their life, what healthy activities can be added, what friendships need to be ended and what new friendships should be established and cultivated, and what unhealthy habits need to be replaced with good routines.

_____

_____

_____

_____

_____

_____

_____

Now pray over your plan and ask God to give you wisdom to help guard and protect your child. *"Call to Me, and I will answer you, and show you great and mighty things, which you do not know."* (Jeremiah 33:3)

BIBLIOGRAPHY

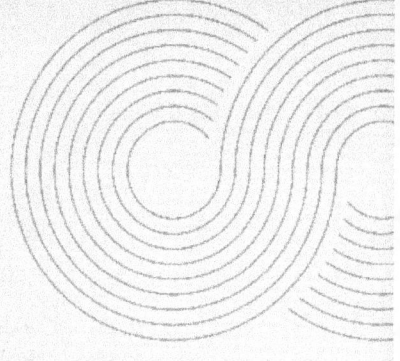

Bohlin, Sue. "The Darkness of Twilight: A Christian Perspective". June 27, 2010. https://probe.org

Children's Health. Health & Wellness Library. "Elf on the Shelf: Christmas friend or foe?" www.childrens.com/health-wellness/featured-content. Accessed May 2023.

Definitions from Merriam Webster. Google.com.

Definitions from Oxford Languages. Google.com.

Ferris, Will John-Michael. "10 Darkest Fairy Tales." June 12, 2019. Listverse.com/2019/06/12/10-darkest-fairy-tales.

"God Freed Me From Gaming Addiction." April 6, 2013. https://testimonyshare.com

Gracey, James. "50 Shades of Red: Sexuality and Loss of Innocence in Little Red Riding Hood". August 3, 2017. Folklorethursday.com.

"Greek Mythology". Encyclopedia Britannica, Inc. Published August 23, 2022. https://www.britannica.comhttps://www.britannica.com/topic/Greek-mythology

"Halloween." Updated March 28, 2023 by history.com editors. History.com/topics/Halloween/history-of-Halloween.

Hempe, Melanie.. "What to do When Your Child is Addicted to Video Games". April 24, 2023. https://www.thegospelcoalition.org

KJV with Strong's Concordance. Godrules.net.

King James. Amplified. New King James. Amplified Classic. The Voice. Biblegateway.com.

"Obsessive-Compulsive Disorder (OCD)." https://www.hopkinsmedicine.org/health. Accessed July 10, 2023.

"Obsessive-compulsive disorder (OCD)". Mayoclinic.org/diseases-conditions/obsessive-compulsive-disorder/symptoms-causes. Accessed July 10, 2023.

"Parental Concerns About Dungeons and Dragons". Focus on the Family. https://www.focusonthefamily.com. Accessed May 2023.

Pollack, Lauren O. and Forbush, Kelsie T. "Why Do Eating Disorders and Obsessive Compulsive Disorder Co-Occur?" Pub. Online 2013 Feb 13. Doi: 10.1016/j.eatbeh.2013.01.004. Retrieved from National Library of Medicine. Ncbi/nlm.gov/pmc/articles.

"Santa Claus." Updated April 20, 2023 by history.com editors. History.com/topics/Christmas/santa-claus.

"Saturnalia." Updated September 14, 2022 by history.com editors. History.com/topics/ancient-rome/saturnalia.

Tarbox, Phyllis. "Praying Deliverance for Small Children". Aandbcounseling.com/praying-deliverance-for-small-children/. Accessed June 2023.

White magic. Gotquestions.org.

"Witchcraft: What Christian Parents Need to Know". Focusonthefamily.com/parenting/witchcraft-what-christian-parents-need-to-know/. Accessed June 2023.

"Zodiac Signs: Learn the Names, Symbols, and More!" January 21, 2022. Dictionary.com.

About
Kharis Publishing:

Kharis Publishing, an imprint of Kharis Media LLC, is a leading Christian and inspirational book publisher based in Aurora, Chicago metropolitan area, Illinois. Kharis' dual mission is to give voice to under-represented writers (including women and first-time authors) and equip orphans in developing countries with literacy tools. That is why, for each book sold, the publisher channels some of the proceeds into providing books and computers for orphanages in developing countries so that these kids may learn to read, dream, and grow. For a limited time, Kharis Publishing is accepting unsolicited queries for nonfiction (Christian, self-help, memoirs, business, health and wellness) from qualified leaders, professionals, pastors, and ministers. Learn more at: https://kharispublishing.com/

www.ingramcontent.com/pod-product-compliance
Lightning Source LLC
Chambersburg PA
CBHW070154100426
42743CB00013B/2911